FIJI

TRAVEL GUIDE 2024 - 2025

The Ultimate Resource for Itineraries, Transportation, Where to Stay, What to See, Where to Eat, and Insider Tips

Sandi H. Newman

Copyright © 2024 Sandi H. Newman. All rights reserved.

No part of this publication may be reproduced, distributed, or transmitted in any form or by any means, including photocopying, recording, or other electronic or mechanical methods, without the prior written permission of the author, except in the case of brief quotations embodied in critical reviews and certain other noncommercial uses permitted by copyright law.

Disclaimer

The information contained in this book is for general informational purposes only. While the author has made every effort to ensure the accuracy and completeness of the information provided, we make no representations or warranties of any kind, express or implied, about the accuracy, reliability, suitability, or availability with respect to the book or the information, products, services, or related graphics contained in the book for any purpose. Any reliance you place on such information is therefore strictly at your own risk.

The author will not be liable for any false, inaccurate, inappropriate, or incomplete information presented in this book. The author will not be liable for any damages of any kind arising from the use of this book, including but not limited to direct, indirect, incidental, punitive, and consequential damages.

The author does not assume and hereby disclaims any liability to any party for any loss, damage, or disruption caused by errors or omissions, whether such errors or omissions result from negligence, accident, or any other cause.

All information is provided "as is" with no guarantee of completeness, accuracy, timeliness, or of the results obtained from the use of this information, and without warranty of any kind, express or implied, including, but not limited to warranties of performance, merchantability, and fitness for a particular purpose.

This book includes links to other websites for informational purposes only. These links do not signify an endorsement of the content or opinions contained within those websites. The author has no control over the nature, content, and availability of those sites.

Travel information such as visa requirements, transportation schedules, prices, and business operations are subject to change and may vary. It is recommended that travelers verify such information independently.

Any product names, logos, brands, and other trademarks or images featured or referred to within this book are the property of their respective trademark holders. These trademark holders are not affiliated with the author, and they do not sponsor or endorse this book.

The author reserves the right to make changes or updates to the content of this book at any time without prior notice.

By using this book, you agree to the terms of this disclaimer. If you do not agree with any part of this disclaimer, do not use this book.

TABLE OF CONTENTS

THE MAP OF FIJI 9
INTRODUCTION 10
CHAPTER 1 16
THE HISTORY OF FIJI 16
    Why you should Choose Fiji for Your Next Adventure 20
CHAPTER 2 25
PREPARING FOR YOUR TRIP 25
    Visa Requirements and Travel Documents 25
    Best Times to Visit Fiji 28
    Health and Safety Tips 32
    What to Pack for Your Fiji Adventure 36
CHAPTER 2 40
GETTING THERE AND GETTING AROUND 40
    International Flights to Fiji 40
    Domestic Travel: Flights, Ferries, and Car Rentals 43
    Navigating Fiji's Public Transportation System 47
    Local Customs and Etiquette for Travelers 51
CHAPTER 3 55
EXPLORING FIJI'S ISLANDS 55
    Viti Levu 55

Vanua Levu 59
The Mamanuca Islands 64
The Yasawa Islands 67
Taveuni 71
Kadavu 75
Lau Group 80
CHAPTER 4 85
MUST-SEE ATTRACTIONS 85
Sigatoka Sand Dunes National Park 85
Garden of the Sleeping Giant 88
Navua River and Waterfalls 92
Sri Siva Subramaniya Temple 96
Fiji Museum 100
Colo-I-Suva Forest Park 104
Bouma National Heritage Park 107
Nadi's Handicraft Market 112
CHAPTER 5 117
ACTIVITIES FOR EVERY TRAVELER 117
Activities for Solo Travelers 117
Romantic Escapes for Couples 121
Fun for Families with Kids 125
Group Activities for Friends and Families 130

CHAPTER 6 136
ACCOMMODATION OPTIONS 136
Luxury Resorts and Villas 136
Mid-Range Hotels and Lodges 140
Budget-Friendly Hostels and Guesthouses 144
Unique Stays: Bures and Eco-Lodges 148
Best Places to Stay for Different Types of Travelers . 152
CHAPTER 7 157
EXPERIENCING FIJI'S RICH CULTURE 157
Traditional Fijian Ceremonies 157
Fijian Cuisine: What to Try and Where 162
Visiting Local Villages 166
The Art of Fijian Handicrafts 170
Fijian Festivals and Events 174
Basic Fijian Phrases 179
CHAPTER 8 185
BEACHES AND WATER ACTIVITIES 185
Best Beaches for Relaxation 185
Top Spots for Snorkeling and Diving 189
Sailing and Yachting Adventures 193
Kayaking and Paddleboarding 199
Deep-Sea Fishing Excursions 203

CHAPTER 9 209

LAND ADVENTURES AND NATURE 209

   Hiking Trails and Nature Walks 209

   Bird Watching and Wildlife Tours 213

   Visiting Fiji's National Parks 218

   Exploring Caves and Waterfalls 224

   Zip-Lining and Canopy Tours 229

CHAPTER 10 235

WELLNESS AND RELAXATION 235

   Best Spas and Wellness Retreats 235

   Yoga and Meditation in Paradise 240

   Natural Hot Springs and Mud Baths 245

   Healthy Eating and Detox Programs 249

CHAPTER 11 255

SHOPPING AND SOUVENIRS 255

   Markets and Bazaars to Explore 255

   Unique Fijian Souvenirs to Bring Home 256

CHAPTER 12 261

DINING AND NIGHTLIFE 261

   Top Restaurants for Fine Dining 261

   Best Local Eateries for Authentic Fijian Food 265

   Nightlife: Bars, Clubs, and Entertainment 269

Food Festivals and Culinary Events 273
CHAPTER 13 279
PRACTICAL INFORMATION FOR TRAVELERS 279
   Currency and Banking 279
   Communication and Internet Access 284
   Mobile Phone Services 285
   Internet Access 286
   Telecommunications Providers 287
   Practical Tips for Staying Connected 288
   Emergency Contacts and Services 290
   Fire Services 293
CHAPTER 14 297
DAY TRIPS AND EXCURSIONS 297
CONCLUSION 303

THE MAP OF FIJI

Scan the QR code below to be redirected to the map of Fiji.

Click here to be redirected to the map of Fiji.

INTRODUCTION

This travel guide is designed to help you discover the hidden gems, breathtaking sights, and rich history that Fiji has to offer. Whether you are planning your first trip or returning for another visit, this guide aims to provide you with all the information you need to make your journey unforgettable.

Fiji is an archipelago of over 330 islands, each offering its own unique experiences. The two largest islands, Viti Levu and Vanua Levu, are home to most of the population and many of the main tourist attractions. Fiji's islands are known for their stunning beaches, crystal-clear waters, and lush tropical landscapes. But there is so much more to Fiji than its natural beauty.

Fiji has a rich cultural heritage that dates back thousands of years. The Fijian people are known for their warm hospitality and vibrant traditions. When you visit Fiji, you will have the opportunity to experience traditional ceremonies, taste delicious local cuisine, and learn about the history and customs that make this country so unique. Fijians are proud of their culture and love to share it with visitors.

Before you embark on your adventure, it is important to prepare properly. This guide will provide you with essential information about visa requirements, health and safety tips, and what to pack for your trip. Fiji has a tropical climate, so lightweight clothing is recommended, but it is also important to bring items like sunscreen, insect repellent, and comfortable footwear for exploring.

Once you arrive in Fiji, you will find that getting around is relatively easy. The main international airport is located in Nadi, on Viti Levu, and there are regular domestic flights to the other islands. Public transportation is available, but for more flexibility, you might consider renting a car or using local taxis. Understanding local customs and etiquette will also help you navigate your way and make the most of your stay.

Fiji is divided into several regions, each offering its own attractions and activities. Viti Levu, the largest island, is home to the capital city of Suva, where you can explore museums, markets, and cultural sites. The island's Coral Coast and Pacific Harbour are famous for their beautiful beaches and adventure activities like diving, snorkeling, and surfing. Vanua Levu, the second-largest island, is less developed but offers pristine natural beauty and a more laid-back atmosphere.

The Mamanuca and Yasawa Islands are popular destinations for their picturesque scenery and luxury resorts. These islands are perfect for honeymooners and those seeking a romantic getaway. Taveuni, known as the Garden Island, is famous for its lush rainforests and waterfalls, making it a paradise for nature lovers and hikers. Kadavu, with its unspoiled coral reefs, is a top spot for diving enthusiasts.

As you explore Fiji, you will discover many must-see attractions. The Sigatoka Sand Dunes National Park, the Garden of the Sleeping Giant, and the Navua River are just a few of the natural wonders waiting for you. You can visit historical sites like the Sri Siva Subramaniya Temple and the Fiji Museum to learn more about the country's heritage. For a taste of local life, don't miss the vibrant markets in Nadi and Suva.

This guide also offers suggestions for activities tailored to different types of travelers. Solo adventurers can find plenty of hiking trails, diving spots, and surfing locations to explore. Couples can enjoy romantic beach picnics, sunset cruises, and couples' spa treatments. Families will find family-friendly resorts, educational tours, and fun beach activities that kids will love. There are also plenty of group activities, from island-hopping tours to cultural shows, that are perfect for friends traveling together.

When it comes to accommodation, Fiji offers a wide range of options to suit every budget and preference. You can choose from luxury resorts and villas, mid-range hotels and lodges, budget-friendly hostels and guesthouses, or unique stays like traditional bures and eco-lodges. This guide will help you find the best places to stay based on your needs and interests.

Experiencing Fijian culture is a highlight of any visit. You can participate in traditional ceremonies, sample delicious Fijian dishes, visit local villages, and see artisans at work creating beautiful handicrafts. Fijian festivals and events are colorful and lively, offering a great way to immerse yourself in the local culture. Learning a few basic Fijian phrases will also enhance your interactions with the friendly locals.

Fiji's beaches and water activities are world-renowned. Whether you want to relax on a quiet beach, snorkel in vibrant coral reefs, or try your hand at kayaking or paddleboarding, you will find plenty of options. Sailing and yachting are also popular, offering a unique way to explore the islands. For those who enjoy fishing, there are deep-sea fishing excursions available.

Land adventures are just as exciting. Fiji's national parks, hiking trails, and nature walks allow you to explore the islands' diverse ecosystems. Bird watching, wildlife tours, and zip-lining are just a few of the activities that nature lovers will enjoy. For a more relaxed experience, you can visit natural hot springs, mud baths, or enjoy a yoga and meditation retreat.

Shopping in Fiji is a delightful experience. You can explore bustling markets and bazaars, where you will find unique souvenirs to bring home. Handcrafted items like woven baskets, traditional masi cloth, and wooden carvings make wonderful mementos. This guide provides tips on where to shop and how to bargain for the best deals.

Dining in Fiji offers a mix of local and international cuisine. From fine dining restaurants to local eateries, there is something to suit every palate. Fresh seafood, tropical fruits, and traditional Fijian dishes are must-tries. The nightlife in Fiji is vibrant, with bars, clubs, and entertainment options to enjoy.

Practical information is essential for a smooth trip. This guide covers topics like currency and banking, communication and internet access, and emergency contacts and services. Sustainable and responsible travel tips are also included, helping you to minimize your impact on the environment and support local communities

For those looking to explore beyond the main tourist areas, day trips and excursions offer exciting opportunities. You can take cultural and historical tours, visit neighboring islands, or embark on adventure and eco-tours. This guide provides recommendations for the best day trips based on your interests.

To ensure you have a memorable trip, this guide offers tips on what to do and what to avoid in Fiji. Safety tips, advice on how to make the most of your time, and insights into respecting local customs and traditions will help you have an enjoyable and respectful experience.

As you turn the pages of this travel guide, you will find a wealth of information designed to enhance your visit to Fiji. From practical tips to detailed descriptions of attractions and activities, this guide aims to be your comprehensive resource for exploring this beautiful country. Whether you are seeking adventure, relaxation, cultural experiences, or family fun, Fiji has something for everyone. We hope this guide inspires you to discover the magic of Fiji and creates memories that will last a lifetime.

CHAPTER 1

THE HISTORY OF FIJI

Fiji is a beautiful island nation in the South Pacific Ocean, rich in history and culture. The story of Fiji begins about 3,500 years ago when the first settlers arrived. These people, known as the Lapita, were skilled sailors and navigators from Southeast Asia. They traveled great distances in their canoes, guided by the stars, to reach the islands of Fiji. They brought with them their customs, traditions, and skills, which laid the foundation for Fijian culture.

The Lapita people were the ancestors of the Melanesians, who settled in Fiji and developed a complex society. They lived in small villages, practiced agriculture, and were known for their pottery, which featured intricate designs. Over time, these early settlers spread across the islands, establishing communities and interacting with neighboring islanders. This period saw the development of distinct Fijian cultural practices, including traditional dances, music, and art forms that are still celebrated today.

By the 10th century, the influence of the Polynesians became evident in Fiji. The Polynesians brought with them new technologies and customs, blending with the existing Melanesian culture. This fusion of cultures created the unique Fijian identity that is still evident today. The Fijians were known for their impressive seafaring skills, constructing large, double-hulled canoes capable of long voyages. They established trade routes and communication networks with other Pacific islands, exchanging goods, knowledge, and cultural practices.

Fijian society was organized into complex hierarchical systems based on kinship and social status. Chiefs held significant power and were responsible for maintaining order and overseeing the well-being of their people. They governed their territories and led their communities in ceremonies and rituals. Fijian villages were closely knit, with strong communal ties and a deep respect for tradition and authority.

In the early 19th century, European explorers and traders began to arrive in Fiji. The first known European to visit Fiji was the Dutch explorer Abel Tasman in 1643, followed by the British explorer Captain James Cook in 1774. These early encounters were sporadic and did not lead to significant changes in Fijian society. However, by the early 1800s, more Europeans, including missionaries, began to settle in Fiji, bringing with them new ideas, technologies, and religions.

The arrival of Christian missionaries had a profound impact on Fijian society. Led by figures such as Reverend John Hunt and Reverend David Cargill, the missionaries introduced Christianity to the Fijian people. Many Fijians converted to Christianity, and this new faith began to reshape traditional practices and beliefs. The missionaries also played a role in education, establishing schools and promoting literacy among the Fijian population.

During this period, Fiji experienced significant social and political changes. Intertribal warfare, which had been a common aspect of Fijian life, began to decline as Christianity and new social norms spread. The influence of European traders also grew, leading to increased contact with the outside world. The introduction of firearms and other goods altered traditional power dynamics and trade practices.

In 1874, Fiji became a British colony. This marked a new chapter in Fijian history, bringing about major changes in governance, economy, and society. The British colonial administration introduced new laws, systems of land ownership, and economic policies. The colonial government encouraged the development of a plantation economy, primarily focused on sugar cane production. To meet the labor demands of the plantations, the British brought indentured laborers from India to Fiji. This period saw the beginning of the Indian community in Fiji, which has since become an integral part of the country's multicultural society.

The early 20th century was a time of significant development and modernization in Fiji. Infrastructure such as roads, ports, and schools were built, and the economy grew. However, this period also saw social tensions, particularly between the indigenous Fijian and Indian communities. These tensions stemmed from issues such as land ownership, economic competition, and cultural differences.

Fiji gained independence from Britain on October 10, 1970. This was a momentous occasion, marking the end of nearly a century of colonial rule. The newly independent nation faced the challenge of building a unified society that respected the rights and traditions of all its people. The post-independence period saw efforts to create a democratic government and develop the country's economy.

However, Fiji's path to stability was not without difficulties. The country experienced several military coups, the first of which occurred in 1987. These coups were driven by ethnic tensions and political disputes. Despite these challenges, Fiji has made strides towards reconciliation and democracy. The country has held elections, worked to address social inequalities, and promoted cultural understanding.

Today, Fiji is known for its vibrant culture, warm hospitality, and stunning natural beauty. The nation continues to celebrate its diverse heritage, with festivals, traditional ceremonies, and cultural events held throughout the year. Fiji's history is a testament to the resilience and adaptability of its people, who have navigated waves of change while preserving their rich traditions and way of life.

Understanding the history of Fiji provides valuable insights into the country's present and future. The blend of

Melanesian and Polynesian influences, the impact of European colonization, and the contributions of the Indian community have all shaped modern Fiji. As you explore this beautiful nation, you will see how its history is woven into every aspect of daily life, from the traditional crafts sold in markets to the rituals performed in villages.

Fiji's history is a story of discovery, adaptation, and resilience. It is a narrative that continues to evolve, reflecting the dynamic and diverse nature of this island nation. As you journey through Fiji, you will not only witness its breathtaking landscapes and vibrant culture but also gain a deeper appreciation for the historical threads that bind this remarkable country together.

Why you should Choose Fiji for Your Next Adventure

Fiji is an exceptional destination for your next adventure, offering a mix of natural beauty, rich culture, and unique experiences that are hard to find anywhere else. One of the primary reasons to choose Fiji is its stunning natural environment. The country is made up of over 330 islands, each with its own charm. The beaches in Fiji are some of the most beautiful in the world, featuring soft white sand and clear, turquoise waters. Whether you want to relax in the sun, swim in the ocean, or explore underwater life through snorkeling or diving, Fiji's beaches are perfect for all these activities.

The underwater world in Fiji is a major attraction for divers and snorkelers. The Great Astrolabe Reef and the Rainbow Reef are famous for their vibrant coral and diverse marine life. You can see colorful fish, sea turtles, and even sharks in these waters. The clarity of the water and the health of the coral reefs make Fiji one of the best places in the world for underwater exploration. If you have never tried diving before, there are many places in Fiji where you can take a beginner's course and get certified.

Beyond the beaches, Fiji's interior landscapes are equally breathtaking. The islands are covered with lush rainforests, filled with exotic plants and animals. Hiking through these forests is a wonderful way to experience Fiji's natural beauty up close. There are many trails to choose from, ranging from easy walks to challenging hikes. One of the most famous trails is the Lavena Coastal Walk on Taveuni Island, which takes you through a mix of forest and coastline, ending at a beautiful waterfall where you can swim.

Fiji is not just about natural beauty; it also has a rich cultural heritage that is fascinating to explore. The Fijian people are known for their warm hospitality and welcoming nature. When you visit Fiji, you have the opportunity to learn about traditional Fijian customs and participate in local ceremonies. One of the most important customs is the yaqona (or kava) ceremony, where you can drink a traditional beverage made from the root of the kava plant. This ceremony is an important part of Fijian culture and a great way to connect with the local people.

Another cultural highlight is the Meke dance, a traditional Fijian dance that tells stories through music and movement. Watching a Meke performance is a captivating experience, as the dancers wear traditional costumes and perform to the rhythm of drums and chants. Many resorts and villages in Fiji offer Meke performances for visitors, giving you a chance to see this beautiful tradition firsthand.

Fijian cuisine is another reason to choose Fiji for your next adventure. The food in Fiji is a delicious blend of flavors from the Pacific, India, and China. Fresh seafood is a staple, with dishes like kokoda (a Fijian version of ceviche) being very popular. You can also try lovo, a traditional Fijian feast where food is cooked in an underground oven. This method of cooking gives the food a unique, smoky flavor. If you have a sweet tooth, you will enjoy trying local fruits like papaya, mango, and pineapple, which are fresh and abundant.

Fiji offers a range of activities for all types of travelers. If you are looking for adventure, there are plenty of options such as zip-lining, river rafting, and surfing. Fiji's waves are perfect for both beginners and experienced surfers, with many surf schools offering lessons and equipment rental. For a more relaxed experience, you can take a scenic boat cruise around the islands, visit a spa for a traditional Fijian massage, or simply relax on the beach with a good book.

Families will find Fiji to be an ideal destination as well. Many resorts cater to families with children, offering kids' clubs, family-friendly activities, and babysitting services. You can enjoy activities together, such as visiting the local markets, exploring nature parks, or taking part in cultural workshops. The friendly and safe environment in Fiji makes it a great place for families to bond and create lasting memories.

One of the most special aspects of Fiji is the opportunity to stay in unique accommodations. While there are many luxury resorts, you can also choose to stay in traditional bures, which are Fijian-style cottages. These bures often offer stunning views of the ocean or forest and provide a more authentic and intimate experience of Fijian life. There are also eco-lodges that focus on sustainable tourism, allowing you to enjoy your vacation while minimizing your impact on the environment.

Fiji is also a great destination for honeymooners and couples looking for a romantic getaway. The natural beauty, coupled with the luxurious accommodations and personalized services offered by many resorts, creates the perfect setting for romance. You can enjoy private beach dinners, couples' spa treatments, and secluded picnics on deserted islands. The tranquil and picturesque environment makes Fiji a dream destination for any romantic occasion.

Getting to Fiji is relatively easy, with direct flights available from several major cities around the world. Once you arrive, the local transportation options make it easy to explore the islands. Domestic flights, ferries, and even private boat charters can take you from one island to another, allowing you to experience the diversity of Fiji's landscapes and cultures.

Fiji's commitment to preserving its natural and cultural heritage is evident in its many conservation projects. Visiting protected areas such as national parks and marine reserves supports these efforts and allows you to see some of the most pristine environments in the world. Learning about and respecting the local customs and traditions during your visit also contributes to the sustainability of Fijian culture.

Choosing Fiji for your next adventure means immersing yourself in a destination that offers something for everyone. Whether you are seeking relaxation, adventure, cultural experiences, or family fun, Fiji has it all. The combination of natural beauty, rich culture, and warm hospitality creates a truly unique and unforgettable travel experience. As you plan your trip, you can look forward to discovering the many hidden gems and wonders that make Fiji such a special place.

CHAPTER 2

PREPARING FOR YOUR TRIP

Visa Requirements and Travel Documents

Traveling to Fiji requires careful planning, especially when it comes to understanding visa requirements and ensuring you have the necessary travel documents.

First and foremost, the most critical document you need for international travel is a valid passport. Make sure your passport is up-to-date and will remain valid for at least six months beyond your planned departure date from Fiji. Many countries, including Fiji, have this requirement to avoid issues if your return travel is delayed for any reason. It's also wise to check that your passport has enough blank pages for entry and exit stamps.

When it comes to visa requirements, Fiji has a straightforward policy for many travelers. Citizens of numerous countries can enter Fiji without a visa for short stays, usually up to four months. This is applicable to countries like the United States, Canada, the United Kingdom, Australia, New Zealand, and most European Union nations. If you are a citizen of one of these countries, you only need a valid passport, a return or onward ticket, and proof of sufficient funds for your stay.

For travelers from countries not on Fiji's visa-exempt list, obtaining a visa before traveling is mandatory. You will need to apply for a visa at a Fijian embassy or consulate in your home country. The application process typically requires you to submit several documents, including a completed visa application form, your passport, passport-sized photos, proof of travel arrangements (like flight bookings), proof of accommodation in Fiji, and evidence of sufficient funds to support yourself during your stay.

Regardless of whether you need a visa, it's important to have proof of accommodation arrangements. This could be a reservation confirmation from a hotel or a letter of invitation from a host if you are staying with friends or family. Immigration officers might ask for this information to ensure you have a place to stay during your visit.

Additionally, having proof of sufficient funds is crucial. This means you should be able to show that you have enough money to cover your expenses while in Fiji. Bank statements, credit card statements, or a letter from your bank can serve as proof. This requirement ensures that you won't face financial difficulties during your stay.

Another essential document is your return or onward travel ticket. Fiji's immigration authorities want to be sure that you intend to leave the country at the end of your stay. This is a standard requirement for many countries to prevent illegal stays. Make sure your travel itinerary is clear and that you have the necessary tickets booked.

It's also wise to consider travel insurance. While not a mandatory requirement, travel insurance is highly recommended. It provides coverage for unexpected events like medical emergencies, trip cancellations, lost luggage, and other travel-related issues. Given the remote location of Fiji and the potential costs of emergency medical treatment and evacuation, having travel insurance can offer peace of mind.

If you are traveling to Fiji for purposes other than tourism, such as work, study, or long-term stay, different visa types and requirements apply. For work, you will need a work permit, which generally requires a job offer from a Fijian employer. For studying, you will need a student visa, which requires acceptance into an educational institution in Fiji. These visas involve more detailed application processes and additional documentation.

For those planning to stay longer than the visa-exempt period or the duration granted by their visa, applying for an extension is possible. Extensions are granted by Fiji's Department of Immigration and typically require a valid reason, such as ongoing studies or extended work contracts. The application for extension must be submitted before your current visa expires, and it involves paying a fee and providing supporting documents.

Traveling with children requires additional documentation. If you are traveling with minors, make sure to carry their birth certificates and any documents proving parental or legal guardianship. If only one parent is traveling with the child, a notarized letter of consent from the other parent is often required, especially if the child's surname differs from the accompanying parent. This measure is in place to prevent child abductions and ensure the safety of minors.

Health-related documents may also be necessary. While Fiji does not have stringent vaccination requirements for travelers from most countries, it's recommended to be up-to-date on routine vaccinations. Depending on your travel itinerary, you may need vaccinations for diseases like hepatitis A, hepatitis B, typhoid, and influenza. If you are coming from a country where yellow fever is present, you may need to show proof of yellow fever vaccination.

For travelers with medical conditions, carrying a letter from your doctor detailing your condition and any prescribed medications is wise. Ensure that your medications are clearly labeled and bring enough supply for your entire stay, as some medications may not be readily available in Fiji. It's also helpful to carry a prescription in case you need a refill.

Best Times to Visit Fiji

Choosing the best time to visit Fiji can greatly enhance your experience and ensure you get the most out of your trip. Fiji's climate is tropical, meaning it's warm and pleasant all year round, but there are some differences in weather patterns throughout the year that can affect your plans.

Understanding these patterns can help you decide when to go.

Fiji experiences two main seasons: the dry season and the wet season. The dry season, which runs from May to October, is considered the best time to visit Fiji. During this period, the weather is cooler and less humid, with average temperatures ranging from 26 to 30 degrees Celsius (79 to 86 degrees Fahrenheit). The skies are mostly clear, and there is less rainfall, making it ideal for outdoor activities like beach outings, hiking, and exploring the islands. The dry season also coincides with the peak tourist season, so you can expect more tourists, but it also means more events and activities are available.

June, July, and August are particularly popular months for visiting Fiji. These months have the least rainfall and the most comfortable temperatures, making them perfect for all kinds of activities, from lounging on the beach to diving and snorkeling in the crystal-clear waters. The cooler temperatures are also great for hiking through Fiji's lush rainforests or visiting cultural sites without the discomfort of excessive heat and humidity. The winds are gentle, which makes it an excellent time for sailing and other water sports.

If you prefer a quieter experience with fewer crowds, the shoulder months of May and October are also excellent times to visit. During these months, the weather is still relatively dry and pleasant, but there are fewer tourists compared to the peak months. You can enjoy the beautiful beaches and tourist attractions without the hustle and bustle, and you may find better deals on accommodations and flights.

The wet season in Fiji lasts from November to April. This period is characterized by higher temperatures and humidity, with average temperatures ranging from 27 to 31 degrees Celsius (81 to 88 degrees Fahrenheit). The wet season brings more frequent rainfall and the possibility of tropical cyclones, especially between January and March. While the rain can be heavy at times, it usually comes in short bursts, often followed by sunshine. The increased humidity can make outdoor activities less comfortable, but it's still possible to enjoy many aspects of Fiji during this season.

One advantage of visiting during the wet season is that it is the off-peak tourist period. This means fewer tourists and more opportunities to experience the islands in a more tranquil setting. Accommodations and flights are often cheaper, and you might find special deals and discounts. The rainforests are lush and vibrant, and the waterfalls are at their most impressive due to the higher water flow. If you don't mind the occasional rain shower, you can still have a fantastic time exploring Fiji's natural beauty.

Another benefit of visiting during the wet season is the opportunity to witness some of Fiji's unique cultural events and festivals. For example, the Hibiscus Festival, held in August, is one of the biggest cultural festivals in Fiji, featuring parades, performances, and various competitions.

Although it falls at the end of the dry season, it's an event worth planning your trip around. During the wet season, you can also experience Fijian Christmas and New Year celebrations, which are rich in local traditions and offer a unique glimpse into the island's culture.

Marine life in Fiji is also abundant during the wet season. The warmer waters attract a variety of marine species, making it a great time for diving and snorkeling. You can see vibrant coral reefs, colorful fish, and even larger marine animals like manta rays and sharks. The visibility underwater might not be as clear as during the dry season, but the diversity of marine life can make up for it.

It's important to consider the regional variations within Fiji as well. The larger islands, such as Viti Levu and Vanua Levu, have more diverse weather patterns due to their size and topography. The eastern sides of these islands tend to receive more rainfall than the western sides. This means that even during the wet season, you might find drier conditions on the western coasts. For instance, Nadi, located on the west coast of Viti Levu, often experiences less rainfall compared to Suva on the east coast.

For those interested in surfing, the best time to visit Fiji is from April to October. During these months, the surf conditions are at their best, with consistent swells and favorable winds. Famous surf spots like Cloudbreak and Namotu Lefts attract surfers from all over the world. Even if you're not a surfer, watching the skilled surfers tackle these impressive waves can be an exciting experience.

Health and Safety Tips

Visiting Fiji can be a wonderful experience, but it is important to be prepared when it comes to health and safety. Knowing what to expect and taking the right precautions can ensure that your trip is enjoyable and worry-free.

First and foremost, make sure you are in good health before you travel. It is a good idea to visit your doctor for a check-up and discuss any health concerns you might have. Tell your doctor about your travel plans so they can advise you on any vaccinations or medications you might need. For Fiji, there are no mandatory vaccinations, but it is recommended to be up-to-date on routine vaccinations such as measles, mumps, and rubella (MMR), diphtheria, tetanus, and pertussis (DTP), and influenza. Depending on your travel itinerary, you might also consider vaccines for hepatitis A, hepatitis B, typhoid, and influenza.

It is also wise to consider travel insurance that covers medical emergencies. Medical care in Fiji can be expensive, especially if you need to be evacuated to another country for treatment. Travel insurance can help cover these costs and provide peace of mind. Make sure your insurance policy covers all the activities you plan to do, such as diving or hiking.

When you arrive in Fiji, one of the first things to remember is to stay hydrated. Fiji's tropical climate can be quite hot and humid, especially during the wet season. Drink plenty of bottled or boiled water to avoid dehydration. Tap water in urban areas like Nadi and Suva is generally safe to drink, but it is better to stick to bottled water in rural areas to avoid any risk of waterborne diseases.

Be mindful of what you eat. While Fijian food is delicious, it is important to make sure it is properly cooked and served hot. Avoid raw or undercooked seafood, and be cautious with street food, as it might not always meet the same hygiene standards you are used to. Fruits and vegetables should be peeled or thoroughly washed. This can help prevent stomach upset or more serious illnesses caused by bacteria or parasites.

Mosquitoes can be a nuisance in Fiji, and they can carry diseases such as dengue fever and Zika virus. Protect yourself by using insect repellent containing DEET, wearing long sleeves and pants, and sleeping under mosquito nets if you are staying in areas where mosquitoes are prevalent. It is also helpful to stay in accommodations that are air-conditioned or have good mosquito screens on windows and doors.

Sun protection is essential in Fiji, as the sun can be very strong. Wear sunscreen with a high SPF, a wide-brimmed hat, and sunglasses to protect your skin and eyes. Reapply sunscreen regularly, especially after swimming or sweating.

It is also a good idea to seek shade during the hottest parts of the day, usually between 10 a.m. and 4 p.m., to avoid sunburn and heatstroke.

If you plan to spend time in the ocean, be aware of the risks associated with water activities. The waters around Fiji are generally safe, but it is important to be cautious. Always swim in designated areas and heed any warnings about strong currents or dangerous marine life. If you are snorkeling or diving, be mindful of coral reefs and marine animals. Do not touch or disturb them, as some can be harmful or even deadly. Always follow the guidance of experienced instructors and use proper equipment.

Another important aspect of health and safety in Fiji is personal security. Fiji is generally a safe destination, but it is wise to take common-sense precautions. Keep your valuables secure and avoid displaying expensive items like jewelry or electronics. Use hotel safes for passports, money, and other important documents. Be cautious when withdrawing money from ATMs and try to do so during the day and in busy, well-lit areas.

When exploring the islands, especially in remote areas, it is important to let someone know your plans. Inform your hotel or a friend about your itinerary and expected return time. This is especially important if you are hiking or visiting less populated islands. Carry a basic first aid kit with items like bandages, antiseptic wipes, and pain relievers, as well as any personal medications you might need.

Road safety is another important consideration. If you plan to rent a car, make sure you are familiar with local driving laws and conditions. In Fiji, people drive on the left side of the road, and roads can be narrow and winding, especially in rural areas. Always wear your seatbelt, obey speed limits, and avoid driving at night if possible, as road lighting can be poor and animals or pedestrians might be on the road.

If you are traveling during the wet season, be aware of the risk of cyclones and heavy rainfall. Cyclone season in Fiji runs from November to April. It is important to stay informed about weather conditions and heed any warnings or advice from local authorities. If a cyclone is approaching, follow the guidance provided by your accommodation and local emergency services. Having a basic emergency kit with essentials like water, non-perishable food, a flashlight, and batteries can be helpful.

Understanding local customs and traditions can also contribute to your safety and well-being in Fiji. Fijians are known for their hospitality and friendliness, but it is important to respect their culture. Dress modestly when visiting villages, cover your shoulders and knees, and remove your hat when indoors. When participating in traditional ceremonies, follow the lead of your hosts and show respect.

Lastly, keep in mind that medical facilities in Fiji can vary in quality. Major cities like Suva and Nadi have hospitals and clinics that offer a range of medical services, but facilities in rural areas might be more basic. If you have a serious health condition, it is a good idea to carry a letter from your doctor detailing your condition and any required medications. Bring enough medication for your entire stay, as some medicines might not be available in Fiji.

What to Pack for Your Fiji Adventure

Packing for a trip to Fiji requires careful thought to ensure you have everything you need for a comfortable and enjoyable experience. This guide will help you understand what to pack for your Fiji adventure, keeping it straightforward and easy to comprehend.

First and foremost, consider the tropical climate of Fiji. The weather is generally warm and humid, so lightweight, breathable clothing is essential. Pack plenty of T-shirts, shorts, and light dresses made from natural fabrics like cotton or linen. These materials help keep you cool and comfortable in the heat. If you plan to visit during the cooler dry season, which runs from May to October, you might also want to bring a few lightweight long-sleeve shirts and pants for cooler evenings.

Swimwear is a must when visiting Fiji. You will likely spend a lot of time at the beach or by the pool, so pack at least two swimsuits. This way, you can have one drying while you wear the other. If you plan to do any snorkeling, diving, or other water sports, consider bringing a rash guard or swim shirt for added sun protection.

Sun protection is crucial in Fiji due to the strong tropical sun. Pack a high-SPF sunscreen, ideally water-resistant, to protect your skin from sunburn. Don't forget lip balm with SPF as well. A wide-brimmed hat and good-quality sunglasses are also essential to protect your face and eyes from the sun's harsh rays. It's also helpful to bring after-sun lotion or aloe vera gel to soothe your skin if you do get too much sun.

Footwear should be practical and comfortable. Pack a pair of flip-flops or sandals for the beach and casual wear. For activities like hiking or exploring the islands, bring sturdy walking shoes or sneakers. Water shoes can be useful if you plan to walk on rocky beaches or coral reefs. They protect your feet and provide better traction in slippery conditions.

Insect repellent is another important item to pack. Mosquitoes can be quite active in Fiji, especially in the evenings and near water. Choose a repellent with DEET or another effective ingredient to protect yourself from bites. If you are particularly sensitive to insect bites, consider bringing an anti-itch cream or antihistamine tablets.

Toiletries and personal care items are essential, but it's best to pack travel-sized versions to save space. Bring basics like toothpaste, toothbrush, shampoo, conditioner, soap, and deodorant. If you wear contact lenses, don't forget your lens solution and a spare pair of lenses. Feminine hygiene products may not be readily available in remote areas, so bring enough to last your entire trip. It's also a good idea to pack a small first aid kit with band-aids, antiseptic wipes, pain relievers, and any prescription medications you need.

For technology and electronics, pack your smartphone and charger. An international adapter is necessary if your devices have different plug types from those used in Fiji. A portable power bank can be very useful for keeping your devices charged while on the go. If you plan to capture the beauty of Fiji, don't forget your camera and extra memory cards. A waterproof case or camera can be a great investment for taking photos and videos underwater.

If you plan to explore Fiji's underwater world, consider bringing your snorkeling gear. While you can rent equipment in many places, having your own mask, snorkel, and fins ensures a better fit and comfort. If you are an avid diver, you might also want to bring your diving gear. Don't forget a good-quality dry bag to keep your belongings safe and dry during water activities.

Reading materials can make your downtime more enjoyable. Whether it's a book, e-reader, or travel guide, having something to read while relaxing on the beach or during travel can be very pleasant. If you prefer listening to music or podcasts, don't forget your headphones.

When packing for your trip to Fiji, it's important to be mindful of cultural norms. Fijians are generally conservative, especially in villages and rural areas. Pack modest clothing to wear when visiting villages or attending cultural ceremonies. Women should bring skirts or dresses that cover the knees, and men should have long pants. A sarong can be a versatile item, serving as a cover-up at the beach or a modest wrap when needed.

Reusable items can help you minimize waste and support Fiji's efforts to protect the environment. Bring a reusable water bottle to stay hydrated and reduce plastic waste. A reusable shopping bag can be handy for carrying souvenirs or groceries. If you enjoy coffee or tea, consider bringing a reusable travel mug.

Finally, keep your travel documents safe and organized. Bring your passport, visa (if required), travel insurance documents, and copies of your flight and accommodation bookings. It's a good idea to have both physical copies and digital backups stored in your email or cloud storage. A small travel wallet or organizer can help keep these important documents secure and easily accessible.

CHAPTER 2

GETTING THERE AND GETTING AROUND

International Flights to Fiji

Traveling to Fiji from various parts of the world involves understanding the international flight routes that connect this beautiful island nation to major cities globally. Fiji is an accessible destination, thanks to its well-connected international airports, primarily Nadi International Airport (NAN), which is the main gateway for international travelers.

Nadi International Airport, located on the western side of Viti Levu, is the busiest airport in Fiji and serves as the primary hub for international flights. It is equipped with modern facilities and offers a range of services to ensure a smooth travel experience. Several major airlines operate flights to Nadi, making it a convenient entry point for visitors from around the world.

For travelers from North America, there are several options for direct flights to Fiji. Fiji Airways, the national airline of Fiji, operates direct flights from Los Angeles (LAX) and San Francisco (SFO) to Nadi. These flights typically take around 10 to 11 hours. Air New Zealand also offers flights from Los

Angeles to Nadi, often with a layover in Auckland. The direct flights from these major US cities make it relatively easy for travelers from the United States to reach Fiji.

Travelers from Canada can take advantage of flights from Vancouver (YVR) to Nadi. While there may not be direct flights from Canada, connecting flights through Los Angeles or San Francisco with Fiji Airways are a popular choice. This route usually involves a layover in the United States, providing convenient access for Canadian travelers.

For those traveling from Europe, reaching Fiji involves one or more layovers. Popular routes include flying from major European hubs such as London (LHR), Paris (CDG), or Frankfurt (FRA) to either Los Angeles or Hong Kong, and then taking a connecting flight to Nadi. Airlines such as British Airways, Air France, and Lufthansa offer flights to these hubs, where passengers can then connect with Fiji Airways or other airlines for the final leg of their journey. The total travel time from Europe to Fiji can vary significantly depending on the layover durations and routes chosen, but it typically ranges from 24 to 30 hours.

Australia and New Zealand are among the closest neighbors to Fiji, making flights from these countries frequent and relatively short. From Australia, direct flights to Nadi are available from cities like Sydney (SYD), Melbourne (MEL), and Brisbane (BNE). Qantas, Virgin Australia, and Fiji Airways are the primary airlines operating these routes, with flight durations ranging from 4 to 5 hours. From New

Zealand, Air New Zealand and Fiji Airways offer direct flights from Auckland (AKL), Wellington (WLG), and Christchurch (CHC) to Nadi, with a flight time of about 3 to 4 hours.

Travelers from Asia have several options for reaching Fiji. Direct flights are available from Hong Kong (HKG) and Singapore (SIN) to Nadi, operated by Fiji Airways. These flights provide a convenient link between Asia and Fiji, with flight durations of approximately 10 to 11 hours. Additionally, travelers from other major Asian cities such as Tokyo, Beijing, and Bangkok can reach Fiji by connecting through Hong Kong, Singapore, or Australia.

For those traveling from the Middle East, routes typically involve one or more layovers. Airlines such as Emirates and Qatar Airways offer flights from Dubai (DXB) and Doha (DOH) to major hubs like Sydney, Auckland, or Los Angeles, where passengers can then connect to Fiji Airways flights to Nadi. The total travel time from the Middle East to Fiji can be quite lengthy, often exceeding 24 hours, but these routes provide viable options for travelers from this region.

When planning a trip to Fiji, it is essential to consider the flight schedules and availability. Fiji Airways, being the national carrier, offers the most comprehensive schedule of flights to Nadi, with multiple flights per week from various international destinations. Other airlines such as Qantas, Air New Zealand, Virgin Australia, and Cathay Pacific also contribute to the network of flights connecting Fiji to the world.

Booking flights to Fiji well in advance is recommended, especially during peak travel seasons, which include the dry season from May to October and the holiday periods in December and January. These times of the year see an influx of tourists, and flights can fill up quickly. Additionally, booking early can help secure better fares and preferred travel dates.

In terms of entry requirements, travelers should ensure they have the necessary travel documents. A valid passport with at least six months of validity from the date of entry is required. Depending on your nationality, you may also need a visa to enter Fiji. Many countries are eligible for visa-free entry for short stays, but it is advisable to check the latest visa requirements with the Fijian immigration authorities or your local Fijian embassy.

Domestic Travel: Flights, Ferries, and Car Rentals

Traveling around Fiji involves understanding the different modes of domestic transportation available, including flights, ferries, and car rentals. Each option offers unique advantages and can significantly enhance your experience in this beautiful island nation.

Fiji is an archipelago consisting of over 330 islands, with the two largest islands being Viti Levu and Vanua Levu. These islands are the main hubs for transportation and have the most developed infrastructure. Nadi and Suva, located on Viti Levu, are the primary points of entry and serve as the starting points for most travelers. To explore the rest of Fiji, you will need to consider various transportation methods.

Domestic flights are the quickest and most convenient way to travel between the islands. Fiji Link, a subsidiary of Fiji Airways, is the main domestic airline operating in Fiji. They offer regular flights to many of the larger and more popular islands, such as Taveuni, Kadavu, and the Yasawa and Mamanuca groups. Flights are relatively short, usually taking less than an hour, which makes them a time-efficient option for those who want to maximize their time exploring different islands. Booking flights in advance is recommended, especially during peak travel seasons, to ensure availability and get the best fares.

The small size of the aircraft used for domestic flights means that baggage allowances might be more limited compared to international flights. It is important to check the baggage policy of the airline beforehand to avoid any surprises. Additionally, the scenic views from these flights are often spectacular, providing a unique perspective of Fiji's diverse landscapes and stunning turquoise waters.

Ferries and boats are another popular mode of transportation in Fiji, particularly for reaching the smaller islands that do not have airports. Several ferry companies operate regular services connecting the main islands with the outer islands. One of the main ferry operators is the Yasawa Flyer, which provides daily services to the Yasawa and Mamanuca islands. This ferry is known for its reliability and comfort, making it a preferred choice for many tourists.

Traveling by ferry offers a different experience compared to flying. It allows you to enjoy the journey itself, taking in the breathtaking views of the ocean and the islands along the way. The ferries are generally equipped with amenities such as air-conditioned cabins, snack bars, and comfortable seating, ensuring a pleasant journey. However, ferry schedules can be affected by weather conditions, so it is advisable to check the schedule and plan accordingly.

For those who enjoy more flexibility and independence, renting a car is a great option for exploring Fiji's main islands, particularly Viti Levu and Vanua Levu. Car rentals are widely available at the main airports and in major towns. Companies like Avis, Budget, and Thrifty offer a range of vehicles to suit different needs and budgets. Renting a car allows you to explore at your own pace, visit remote areas that are not easily accessible by public transport, and discover hidden gems off the beaten path.

Driving in Fiji is relatively straightforward, but there are some important things to keep in mind. In Fiji, people drive on the left side of the road, and the speed limits are typically 50 km/h in urban areas and 80 km/h on highways. The roads in urban areas and major tourist routes are generally in good condition, but roads in rural areas can be narrow, winding, and less well-maintained. It is important to drive carefully, especially at night, as road lighting can be poor and animals or pedestrians might be on the road.

When renting a car, make sure to have a valid driver's license. An international driving permit is not required for most travelers, but it is always a good idea to check with the rental company. Familiarize yourself with the rental terms and conditions, including insurance coverage and fuel policy. It is also advisable to inspect the car for any existing damage before driving off and report it to the rental company to avoid any issues later.

For those who prefer not to drive, taxis and private transfers are readily available in Fiji. Taxis are a convenient way to get around towns and cities, and they can also be hired for longer trips. It is best to agree on the fare before starting the journey, as not all taxis have meters. Many hotels and resorts offer airport transfers and can arrange private transportation for tours and excursions, providing a hassle-free option for getting around.

Buses are another affordable and widely used mode of transportation in Fiji, particularly on the main islands. The bus network connects major towns and cities, and there are both local and express services available. Local buses are a budget-friendly way to travel, offering a glimpse into everyday life in Fiji. Express buses are faster and more comfortable, making fewer stops along the way. While buses might not be the fastest option, they are a great way to experience the local culture and interact with the friendly Fijian people.

For those traveling to more remote areas or smaller islands, charter boats and water taxis offer a flexible and personalized mode of transportation. These services can be arranged through local operators or through your accommodation. Chartering a boat allows you to set your own schedule and explore less-visited parts of Fiji at your own pace. Water taxis are particularly useful for short trips between islands or for reaching destinations not covered by regular ferry services.

Navigating Fiji's Public Transportation System

Navigating Fiji's public transportation system is a vital aspect of experiencing the island nation's culture and daily life. Understanding the various modes of public transport available, their schedules, and how to use them effectively can greatly enhance your travel experience.

Public transportation in Fiji primarily includes buses, minibuses, and taxis. These modes of transport are widely used by locals and provide a cost-effective way for tourists to get around. The bus system is the backbone of public transportation in Fiji, covering major towns, cities, and even rural areas. Buses are a common sight on the roads and are the most affordable way to travel across the islands.

Buses in Fiji are operated by several companies, with the largest being the Fiji Bus Operators Association. There are two main types of bus services: local buses and express buses. Local buses are the most common and make frequent stops along their routes, allowing passengers to get on and off at various points. These buses are usually older models and may not have air conditioning, but they offer an authentic experience of daily life in Fiji. Local bus fares are very affordable, and tickets can be purchased on board from the conductor. It is important to carry small change, as drivers and conductors may not always have change for larger bills.

Express buses, on the other hand, are more modern and comfortable, making fewer stops and traveling faster between major towns and cities. These buses are ideal for longer journeys, such as traveling from Nadi to Suva, the capital city. Express buses are usually equipped with air conditioning and more comfortable seating, making the journey more pleasant. Tickets for express buses can be purchased at bus stations or directly from the driver, depending on the service. It is advisable to arrive at the bus station early, especially during peak travel times, to secure a seat.

In addition to the regular bus services, minibuses are another popular mode of public transport in Fiji. Minibuses are smaller vans that operate on fixed routes, similar to buses, but with more flexibility in terms of stopping points. They are faster than local buses and often preferred for shorter trips or routes that are not well-served by the larger bus companies. Minibuses are known for their informal nature; passengers can flag them down anywhere along their route, and they will stop to pick up or drop off. Fares are slightly higher than those of local buses but still very reasonable. Minibuses can be a good option for travelers looking for a quicker and more convenient way to get around.

Taxis are widely available in Fiji and provide a convenient mode of transport, especially in urban areas like Nadi, Suva, and Lautoka. Taxis can be hailed on the street, found at designated taxi stands, or booked in advance through your hotel or a taxi company. It is common practice to agree on the fare before starting the journey if the taxi does not have a meter. Taxis are relatively affordable, but fares can vary depending on the time of day and the distance traveled. For longer trips, such as traveling between cities, it is advisable to negotiate a fixed fare.

For those who prefer more personalized transportation, private hire vehicles and ride-sharing services are available in some parts of Fiji. Companies like Dial-A-Cab and other local operators offer private hire vehicles that can be booked for specific trips or by the hour. These services are more expensive than regular taxis but offer a higher level of comfort and convenience.

When using public transportation in Fiji, it is important to be aware of the schedules and routes. Bus schedules can vary, especially in rural areas, where services may be less frequent. Most bus services start early in the morning and run until the evening, but it is advisable to check the timings in advance. Bus timetables are usually available at bus stations or from the bus company's office. It is also helpful to ask locals or hotel staff for information on bus schedules and the best routes to take.

Navigating the bus system can be straightforward if you keep a few tips in mind. Always look for the bus number and destination displayed on the front of the bus. If you are unsure, ask the driver or conductor to confirm that the bus is going to your intended destination. Be prepared for the possibility of crowded buses during peak times, such as early mornings and late afternoons when people are commuting to and from work.

Safety is another important aspect to consider when using public transportation in Fiji. Generally, public transport is safe, but it is always wise to take basic precautions. Keep an eye on your belongings and avoid carrying large amounts of cash or valuable items. If traveling late at night, it is better to use a taxi or private hire vehicle for added security.

For travelers looking to explore the outer islands, ferries and boats are the primary means of public transportation. Several ferry operators provide services between the main islands and smaller outer islands. Companies like South Sea Cruises and Awesome Adventures Fiji offer regular ferry services to popular destinations such as the Mamanuca and Yasawa Islands. Ferry schedules can be affected by weather conditions, so it is important to check for any updates or changes before traveling. Tickets for ferries can be purchased online, at the ferry terminal, or through travel agents.

Local Customs and Etiquette for Travelers

Understanding and respecting local customs and etiquette is crucial when visiting Fiji. The Fijian culture is rich and deeply rooted in tradition, with a strong emphasis on community, respect, and hospitality.

Fijians are known for their warm and welcoming nature. When you arrive in Fiji, you will likely be greeted with a friendly "Bula!" This greeting means "hello" and is used widely across the islands. Responding with a cheerful "Bula!" is a great way to show friendliness and start your interactions on a positive note.

Respect for elders and those in authority is a significant aspect of Fijian culture. When meeting someone older or in a position of respect, it is customary to bow your head slightly. Shaking hands is common, but for men, a light touch on the shoulder or an arm around the shoulder can accompany the handshake. For women, a gentle handshake is appropriate. Always use your right hand for greeting and giving or receiving items, as the left hand is considered impolite.

When visiting a Fijian village, there are specific customs to follow. One of the most important is the Sevusevu ceremony. This traditional ceremony involves presenting a gift of kava root to the village chief as a sign of respect. Kava is a plant used to make a traditional drink with sedative and anesthetic properties. Participating in a kava ceremony is a unique cultural experience, but it is essential to follow the lead of your hosts. Sit cross-legged on the floor, accept the drink with both hands, and clap once before and three times after drinking.

Dress modestly when visiting villages or attending ceremonies. For men, this means wearing a shirt and long trousers or a sulu (a traditional Fijian sarong). For women, it means wearing a dress or skirt that covers the knees and a top that covers the shoulders. Avoid wearing hats or sunglasses in the village, as these are considered disrespectful. It is also polite to remove your shoes before entering someone's home.

In Fiji, touching someone's head is considered disrespectful, as the head is regarded as the most sacred part of the body. Avoid touching people on the head, even children, and be mindful of your body language. Pointing at people or gesturing with your feet is also considered impolite. When sitting, try to avoid pointing the soles of your feet towards others.

Mealtime in Fiji is often a communal affair, with food being shared among family and friends. If you are invited to a meal, it is polite to wait until the host begins eating before you start. It is also courteous to try a little bit of everything offered, even if you are not familiar with the dishes. Fijians are proud of their cuisine, and showing appreciation for their food is a great way to build rapport.

When it comes to communication, Fijians value indirectness and politeness. They tend to avoid confrontations and may not always express disagreement directly. If you need to decline an invitation or refuse an offer, do so gently and with a smile. Expressing gratitude and showing appreciation for hospitality is essential. A simple "vinaka" (thank you) goes a long way.

Fijian society is deeply rooted in community and family. The concept of "vanua" is central to their culture, representing the land, the people, and their connection. Understanding this interconnectedness can help you appreciate the importance of community events, gatherings, and ceremonies. Participating in or showing respect for these activities is a way to honor their cultural values.

When traveling in Fiji, it is important to be mindful of environmental conservation, as respect for nature is an integral part of Fijian life. Avoid littering, and try to minimize your environmental footprint. Participate in eco-friendly activities and support local conservation efforts whenever possible. This not only shows respect for the land but also aligns with the values of the local communities.

Religion plays a significant role in Fijian life, with Christianity being the dominant faith. Many Fijians attend church services regularly, especially on Sundays. If you are invited to attend a church service, dress conservatively and follow the congregation's lead. Be respectful of their religious practices and observances.

When visiting markets or shopping for souvenirs, haggling is generally acceptable but should be done politely. Start by asking for the price and then make a reasonable counteroffer. Always keep the negotiation friendly and respectful. Fijians are known for their craftsmanship, and purchasing locally made products supports the local economy and preserves traditional arts and crafts.

Public displays of affection should be kept to a minimum, as Fijian culture is conservative regarding relationships and physical contact. Holding hands is generally acceptable, but more intimate displays of affection may be frowned upon, especially in rural areas or villages.

Time in Fiji is often referred to as "Fiji time," reflecting a more relaxed and flexible approach to schedules and punctuality. While this laid-back attitude can be refreshing, it is important to be patient and understanding if things do not always run on a strict schedule. Embrace the slower pace and enjoy the opportunity to immerse yourself in the island way of life.

CHAPTER 3

EXPLORING FIJI'S ISLANDS

Viti Levu

Exploring Viti Levu, the largest island in Fiji, is an adventure that offers a blend of vibrant culture, stunning natural beauty, and diverse activities. This island is not only the political and economic center of Fiji but also a treasure trove of experiences waiting to be discovered. Whether you are interested in history, nature, or simply enjoying the tropical atmosphere, Viti Levu has something for everyone.

The island is home to the capital city, Suva, which is a bustling metropolis with a rich colonial history. Suva is an excellent starting point for exploring Viti Levu. The city offers a mix of modern amenities and traditional Fijian culture. One of the highlights is the Fiji Museum, located in Thurston Gardens. This museum provides an extensive overview of Fijian history and culture, showcasing artifacts that date back over 3,700 years. Walking through the exhibits, you can learn about the island's indigenous heritage, the arrival of Europeans, and the development of modern Fiji.

Suva also boasts vibrant markets where you can experience the local way of life. The Suva Municipal Market is one of the largest markets in Fiji, offering a variety of fresh produce, seafood, and traditional Fijian handicrafts. Strolling through the market, you can taste tropical fruits, purchase handcrafted souvenirs, and interact with friendly local vendors.

For nature enthusiasts, the Colo-I-Suva Forest Park is a must-visit. Located just outside Suva, this lush rainforest park is a haven for hikers and bird watchers. The park features several trails that wind through the forest, leading to natural swimming pools and waterfalls. The serene environment and the sounds of birds and rushing water create a peaceful retreat from the city's hustle and bustle.

Traveling west from Suva, you will reach the Coral Coast, a stretch of coastline known for its beautiful beaches and resorts. The Coral Coast is famous for its crystal-clear waters, making it a perfect destination for snorkeling and diving. The coral reefs teem with marine life, including colorful fish, sea turtles, and occasionally, reef sharks. Many resorts along the coast offer snorkeling and diving tours, providing equipment and guidance for both beginners and experienced divers.

A notable attraction on the Coral Coast is the Sigatoka Sand Dunes National Park. This park is Fiji's first national park and features impressive sand dunes that rise up to 60 meters high. The dunes are an important archaeological site, with excavations revealing ancient artifacts and human remains that provide insight into Fiji's early inhabitants. Visitors can explore the dunes through guided tours, which offer a combination of stunning scenery and historical context.

Continuing along the southern coast, you will find the town of Sigatoka, known as the "Salad Bowl of Fiji" due to its fertile farmland. Sigatoka is a great place to experience Fijian rural life and taste fresh local produce. The Sigatoka River Safari is a popular activity, where you can take a jet boat tour up the Sigatoka River to visit traditional Fijian villages. The tour includes a village visit, where you can participate in a traditional kava ceremony, enjoy local food, and learn about Fijian customs and lifestyle.

Heading further west, you arrive in Nadi, one of Fiji's major tourism hubs. Nadi is home to the country's main international airport, making it a common entry point for visitors. The town itself offers a variety of attractions, including the famous Sri Siva Subramaniya Temple, the largest Hindu temple in the Southern Hemisphere. This colorful temple is an architectural marvel and a center of Hindu worship in Fiji. Visitors are welcome to explore the temple grounds and learn about its significance.

Just outside Nadi is the Garden of the Sleeping Giant, a beautiful botanical garden founded by the late actor Raymond Burr. The garden is known for its extensive collection of orchids and tropical plants. Walking through the garden, you can admire the vibrant flowers, tranquil lily ponds, and the lush greenery that surrounds the area. It is a perfect spot for a relaxing afternoon amid nature's beauty.

Nadi is also the gateway to the Mamanuca and Yasawa Islands, a group of islands known for their stunning beaches and clear waters. Day trips and excursions to these islands are readily available from Nadi, offering opportunities for snorkeling, diving, and simply relaxing on pristine beaches.

For a taste of adventure, head inland to the Nausori Highlands. This region offers rugged landscapes, traditional villages, and breathtaking views. Hiking in the Nausori Highlands allows you to experience Fiji's natural beauty up close, with trails that lead through dense forests, across rivers, and up to high vantage points with panoramic views of the island.

One of the unique features of Viti Levu is its geothermal activity. The Sabeto Hot Springs and Mud Pool, located near Nadi, are a popular destination for those looking to relax and rejuvenate. Visitors can soak in the warm mineral-rich waters and apply therapeutic mud, which is believed to have healing properties. The experience is both relaxing and invigorating, offering a natural spa experience amid a picturesque setting.

Another significant site is the village of Navala, one of the last remaining traditional Fijian villages with thatched bures (huts). Located in the highlands of Ba, Navala offers a glimpse into traditional Fijian architecture and way of life. The villagers are welcoming, and visitors can learn about their customs, participate in traditional activities, and enjoy the scenic beauty of the surrounding mountains.

Exploring Viti Levu also means enjoying its culinary delights. Fijian cuisine is a fusion of indigenous Fijian, Indian, Chinese, and European influences. Fresh seafood, tropical fruits, and root vegetables like taro and cassava are staples. Traditional dishes such as kokoda (raw fish marinated in coconut milk and lime), lovo (a feast cooked in an underground oven), and roti with curry reflect the island's diverse culinary heritage. Many local restaurants and food stalls offer these dishes, providing a delicious way to experience Fijian culture.

As you travel around Viti Levu, you will notice the strong sense of community and hospitality that defines Fijian society. Whether you are visiting a bustling town, a serene beach, or a remote village, the warmth and friendliness of the Fijian people will make your experience memorable. Engaging with locals, participating in cultural activities, and respecting local customs will enrich your understanding of Fiji and create lasting memories.

Vanua Levu

Exploring Vanua Levu, the second-largest island in Fiji, is a journey into a place that offers a unique blend of natural beauty, rich culture, and outdoor adventure. Vanua Levu is less developed and less touristy compared to Viti Levu, making it an ideal destination for those looking to experience a more authentic and serene side of Fiji.

Vanua Levu is known for its lush landscapes, clear waters, and welcoming communities. The main entry point to the island is through Labasa or Savusavu, the two largest towns on the island. Savusavu, often referred to as Fiji's "hidden paradise," is located on the southern coast and is a charming town that serves as a perfect base for exploring the island.

Savusavu is famous for its natural geothermal hot springs. These hot springs are scattered around the town, and some are even used by locals for cooking. A visit to these hot springs offers a unique and relaxing experience. The hot springs located in the village of Namale are particularly well-known and offer therapeutic benefits. Visitors can soak in these natural baths while enjoying the beautiful surrounding scenery.

The marina in Savusavu is another highlight, attracting yachts from around the world. This picturesque harbor is surrounded by lush hills and offers a range of activities, including sailing, fishing, and snorkeling. The waters around Savusavu are rich in marine life, making it a fantastic spot for diving and snorkeling. Dive sites such as the Namena Marine Reserve are renowned for their biodiversity, with vibrant coral reefs and a variety of fish species.

Exploring the interior of Vanua Levu reveals its stunning natural beauty. The island is covered with dense rainforests, rolling hills, and waterfalls. The Wasali Nature Reserve is a must-visit destination for nature lovers. This protected area features several walking trails that lead through the rainforest to stunning viewpoints and waterfalls. The hike to the Wasali Waterfall is particularly rewarding, offering a refreshing swim in the clear pool at the base of the falls.

For those interested in agriculture and local industry, a visit to the copra plantations and sugar cane fields can be enlightening. Copra, the dried meat of coconuts, is a major industry on Vanua Levu. Visiting these plantations provides insight into the traditional methods of copra production and the importance of this industry to the local economy. Similarly, sugar cane farming is prevalent, especially around Labasa, where you can learn about the cultivation and processing of sugar cane.

Labasa, the largest town on Vanua Levu, is located in the northern part of the island. It is an industrial and agricultural hub, known for its sugar mill and vibrant market. The Labasa market is a bustling place where you can find a variety of fresh produce, seafood, and traditional Fijian handicrafts. Exploring the market is a great way to immerse yourself in the local culture and taste some of the island's fresh tropical fruits and traditional foods.

Vanua Levu also offers cultural experiences that allow visitors to connect with the local Fijian way of life. The village of Nukubati is known for its strong cultural heritage and offers visitors the chance to participate in traditional Fijian ceremonies, such as the Sevusevu (kava ceremony). During your visit, you can learn about Fijian customs, traditional dance, and music, and experience the genuine hospitality of the Fijian people.

Another cultural highlight is the celebration of local festivals. The Bula Festival in Labasa is a week-long event filled with cultural performances, traditional dances, and feasting. Attending such a festival provides a deeper understanding of the Fijian community spirit and cultural pride.

For those who love the ocean, Vanua Levu's coastline is dotted with secluded beaches and excellent spots for water sports. The pristine beaches of Jean-Michel Cousteau Resort are particularly noteworthy. This eco-friendly resort is dedicated to marine conservation and offers guests the chance to explore the underwater world through guided dives and snorkeling trips. The resort's marine biologists provide educational sessions about the local marine ecosystem and conservation efforts.

Further along the coast, the Rainbow Reef is one of the world's premier diving locations. Situated between Vanua Levu and Taveuni, the reef is famous for its soft coral gardens and diverse marine life. The Great White Wall, a vertical drop covered in soft white corals, is one of the most iconic dive sites in the area. Diving or snorkeling here is an unforgettable experience, offering a chance to see everything from colorful reef fish to larger pelagic species.

In addition to water activities, Vanua Levu offers opportunities for land-based adventures. The rugged terrain of the island is perfect for hiking and exploring. One of the most popular hikes is to Mount Batini, which provides panoramic views of the island and surrounding ocean. The trek through the rainforest is challenging but rewarding, with the chance to see native wildlife and exotic plants along the way.

Birdwatching is another activity that attracts nature enthusiasts to Vanua Levu. The island is home to several endemic bird species, such as the Silktail and the Orange Dove. Birdwatching tours can be arranged with local guides who are knowledgeable about the best spots to see these unique birds.

If you are interested in marine conservation, Vanua Levu offers several volunteer opportunities. Organizations such as the Marine Ecology Consulting and the Namena Marine Reserve welcome volunteers to assist with coral reef monitoring, turtle conservation, and environmental education programs. Volunteering is a meaningful way to contribute to the preservation of Fiji's natural beauty while gaining a deeper understanding of the island's ecosystem.

For relaxation, Vanua Levu's resorts and spas offer luxurious settings to unwind. Many resorts are located in stunning natural environments, providing breathtaking views and a tranquil atmosphere. Spa treatments often incorporate traditional Fijian techniques and natural ingredients, offering a unique and rejuvenating experience.

The Mamanuca Islands

Exploring the Mamanuca Islands in Fiji offers an unforgettable experience filled with natural beauty, adventure, and relaxation. This archipelago, located to the west of Viti Levu and Nadi, is made up of about 20 small islands, each providing a unique slice of paradise. The Mamanuca Islands are renowned for their crystal-clear waters, stunning coral reefs, and white sandy beaches, making them a top destination for travelers seeking both tranquility and excitement.

When you arrive in the Mamanuca Islands, the first thing you will notice is the breathtaking scenery. The islands are surrounded by turquoise waters that are perfect for swimming, snorkeling, and diving. The vibrant coral reefs teem with marine life, including colorful fish, sea turtles, and even sharks. The clarity of the water and the diversity of the marine ecosystem make snorkeling and diving here an extraordinary experience. For beginners, there are many guided snorkeling tours that provide equipment and instruction, ensuring a safe and enjoyable adventure. Experienced divers can explore deeper reefs and underwater caves, with several dive shops offering advanced diving trips.

One of the most popular activities in the Mamanuca Islands is exploring the reefs. The waters around these islands are home to some of the best coral reefs in the world. Sites like the renowned Namotu Wall and Wilkes Passage offer incredible underwater views and encounters with a variety of sea creatures. For those interested in marine biology, many resorts offer educational programs and guided tours that highlight the importance of coral conservation and the rich biodiversity of the region.

Aside from the underwater attractions, the islands themselves are perfect for exploration. The landscapes are dotted with palm trees, lush vegetation, and volcanic formations. Hiking trails on islands like Malolo and Mana offer scenic views and the chance to experience the local flora and fauna. These hikes can vary in difficulty, from easy walks to more challenging treks, catering to all levels of fitness and adventure.

The Mamanuca Islands are also a paradise for water sports enthusiasts. Windsurfing, kayaking, paddleboarding, and jet skiing are popular activities available at many resorts. The calm lagoons and steady winds provide ideal conditions for these sports, whether you are a novice or an experienced athlete. Many resorts offer equipment rental and lessons, so you can try something new or improve your skills during your stay.

For those who prefer a more leisurely pace, the beaches of the Mamanuca Islands are perfect for relaxation. The soft white sand and gentle waves create a serene environment for sunbathing, reading a book, or simply enjoying the view. Many of the islands have private beaches accessible only to resort guests, ensuring a peaceful and exclusive experience. Beachside bars and restaurants offer refreshing drinks and delicious meals, allowing you to savor the flavors of Fiji while enjoying the coastal scenery.

Cultural experiences are also a highlight of visiting the Mamanuca Islands. The local Fijian communities are known for their hospitality and warmth. Visitors have the opportunity to participate in traditional Fijian ceremonies, such as the kava ceremony, where a drink made from the root of the kava plant is shared. This ritual is an important part of Fijian culture and offers a unique glimpse into local customs. Traditional Fijian dance performances, known as meke, are often held at resorts and provide vibrant displays of storytelling through music and movement.

The Mamanuca Islands have been the setting for several popular movies and television shows, most notably the film "Cast Away" starring Tom Hanks. Monuriki Island, where much of the movie was filmed, is a popular excursion destination. Visitors can take guided tours to the island, explore the filming locations, and enjoy the pristine beauty that made it an ideal movie set. This connection to popular culture adds an interesting dimension to your visit.

Fishing enthusiasts will find the Mamanuca Islands an excellent location for both deep-sea and sport fishing. The waters around the islands are rich with fish such as marlin, tuna, and mahi-mahi. Fishing charters are available for half-day or full-day trips, providing all the necessary equipment and guidance to help you catch the big one. Whether you are an experienced angler or trying fishing for the first time, these trips offer an exciting way to enjoy the ocean.

Accommodation in the Mamanuca Islands ranges from luxury resorts to more budget-friendly options, ensuring that every traveler can find something suitable. High-end resorts offer all-inclusive packages with private villas, fine dining, spa treatments, and personalized services. For those seeking a more affordable stay, there are several mid-range resorts and backpacker-friendly lodges that provide comfortable amenities and access to the same stunning natural beauty.

Sustainability and conservation are important themes in the Mamanuca Islands. Many resorts are committed to eco-friendly practices, such as solar power, water conservation, and waste reduction. These efforts help preserve the pristine environment and ensure that the beauty of the islands can be enjoyed by future generations. Visitors can also participate in conservation activities, such as coral planting and beach clean-ups, making a positive impact during their stay.

The Yasawa Islands

Exploring the Yasawa Islands in Fiji is a journey into an unspoiled paradise that promises pristine beaches, crystal-clear waters, and a deep immersion into the local culture.

The Yasawa Islands are a chain of islands situated northwest of Viti Levu, and they offer a serene and picturesque escape from the more commercialized areas of Fiji.

The Yasawa Islands are known for their stunning natural beauty. The islands are surrounded by clear blue waters that are perfect for swimming, snorkeling, and diving. The underwater world around the Yasawas is teeming with vibrant coral reefs and diverse marine life. Whether you are a seasoned diver or a novice snorkeler, the coral gardens, colorful fish, and gentle manta rays will leave you in awe. One of the most popular snorkeling spots is the Blue Lagoon, which boasts crystal-clear waters and abundant marine life. This lagoon gained fame from the 1980 movie "The Blue Lagoon," and it remains a favorite among visitors.

The Yasawa Islands offer some of the best diving experiences in Fiji. Dive sites such as the Shark Reef Marine Reserve and the Yasawa Islands' coral walls provide opportunities to see a variety of marine species, including sharks, rays, and an array of tropical fish. The warm waters and excellent visibility make diving in the Yasawas a memorable adventure. For those new to diving, there are numerous dive schools that offer courses and guided dives, ensuring a safe and enjoyable experience.

Beyond the underwater attractions, the islands themselves are dotted with secluded beaches and lush landscapes. The white sandy beaches are perfect for sunbathing, beachcombing, and simply relaxing under the tropical sun.

Each island in the Yasawa group has its own unique charm and beauty. For example, Nanuya Levu, also known as Turtle Island, is famous for its luxurious resorts and pristine environment. This private island offers an exclusive experience with activities such as kayaking, paddleboarding, and guided nature walks.

The Yasawa Islands are also rich in cultural experiences. Many of the islands are home to traditional Fijian villages where you can experience the local way of life. Visitors are often welcomed with a traditional kava ceremony, where you can taste the kava drink and learn about its significance in Fijian culture. The villagers are known for their warm hospitality and are eager to share their customs and traditions with visitors. Participating in a village tour provides insight into the daily lives of the Fijian people, their crafts, and their community spirit.

Hiking is another activity that allows you to explore the natural beauty of the Yasawa Islands. The islands' terrain varies from gentle hills to rugged cliffs, offering a range of hiking opportunities. Trails lead through tropical forests, up to high viewpoints with panoramic vistas, and down to hidden beaches. One notable hike is to the summit of Mount Tamasua on Waya Island, which offers stunning views of the surrounding islands and the vast Pacific Ocean. The hike is moderately challenging, but the reward of the breathtaking scenery is well worth the effort.

The Yasawa Islands are also an ideal destination for sailing and island-hopping. Several companies offer sailing tours that take you around the islands, allowing you to explore multiple destinations in a single trip. These tours often include stops at remote beaches, snorkeling spots, and traditional villages. Sailing through the Yasawas provides a unique perspective of the islands and the opportunity to see some of the more secluded and untouched areas.

In terms of accommodation, the Yasawa Islands cater to a range of budgets and preferences. From luxury resorts with private villas and all-inclusive packages to budget-friendly backpacker lodges and campsites, there is something for everyone. Many of the resorts are located on private beaches and offer amenities such as spa services, gourmet dining, and various water sports. For those seeking a more rustic experience, the backpacker lodges provide comfortable accommodations with communal facilities, allowing you to meet fellow travelers and share experiences.

Environmental conservation is an important focus in the Yasawa Islands. Many of the resorts and tour operators are committed to sustainable practices, such as using solar power, reducing plastic waste, and supporting local conservation efforts. Visitors can participate in conservation activities, such as beach clean-ups and coral planting, to help preserve the natural beauty of the islands.

Fishing is another popular activity in the Yasawa Islands. The waters around the islands are rich with fish, making it an excellent spot for both recreational and sport fishing. Fishing charters are available for those who want to try their hand at catching tuna, marlin, or mahi-mahi. The local guides are knowledgeable and provide all the necessary equipment, ensuring an enjoyable fishing experience.

One of the unique aspects of the Yasawa Islands is their relatively untouched and unspoiled environment. Unlike some of the more developed tourist destinations, the Yasawas maintain a sense of tranquility and natural beauty. This makes the islands an ideal destination for those looking to escape the hustle and bustle of everyday life and immerse themselves in a peaceful and pristine setting.

The Yasawa Islands also offer opportunities for wellness and relaxation. Many resorts have spas that offer traditional Fijian massages and treatments using natural ingredients. Yoga and meditation sessions are also available, often held in scenic outdoor settings overlooking the ocean. These wellness activities provide a perfect way to unwind and rejuvenate during your stay.

Taveuni

Exploring Taveuni in Fiji is an experience that brings you closer to nature, culture, and adventure. Known as the "Garden Island" of Fiji, Taveuni is the third-largest island in the country and offers an abundance of natural beauty, from lush rainforests and cascading waterfalls to vibrant coral reefs and pristine beaches.

Taveuni is renowned for its stunning landscapes and rich biodiversity. The island is covered in dense rainforests, home to a variety of flora and fauna that are unique to this part of the world. One of the most significant natural attractions on Taveuni is the Bouma National Heritage Park, which encompasses over 150 square kilometers of protected land. This park is a haven for hikers and nature lovers, with several trails leading through the rainforest to breathtaking viewpoints and waterfalls.

One of the most popular hikes in Bouma National Heritage Park is the trail to the Tavoro Waterfalls. This series of three waterfalls is set amidst lush greenery and offers a refreshing escape from the tropical heat. The first waterfall is easily accessible and features a large pool perfect for swimming. The second and third waterfalls require a bit more effort to reach but reward hikers with stunning views and more secluded swimming spots. The trail is well-marked, and the sound of the waterfalls guides you through the dense forest.

Another highlight within the Bouma National Heritage Park is the Lavena Coastal Walk. This scenic trail takes you along the coast, through villages, and into the rainforest, ending at a beautiful waterfall and natural swimming pool. The walk offers a mix of beach and jungle scenery, and you can see traditional Fijian village life along the way. The trail is relatively easy and can be enjoyed by visitors of all fitness levels. Along the route, you might encounter local wildlife, such as parrots and other tropical birds.

Taveuni is also known for its exceptional diving and snorkeling opportunities. The island is located near the Somosomo Strait, which is famous for its rich marine biodiversity and vibrant coral reefs. One of the most renowned dive sites in the area is the Rainbow Reef, which lives up to its name with its colorful corals and abundant marine life. Diving at the Rainbow Reef offers the chance to see a variety of fish species, including clownfish, angelfish, and parrotfish, as well as larger species such as reef sharks and manta rays. The Great White Wall, a vertical drop covered in soft white corals, is one of the most iconic dive sites at the Rainbow Reef and provides an unforgettable underwater experience.

For those who prefer snorkeling, the waters around Taveuni are equally inviting. The coral gardens near the shore are teeming with marine life, and many resorts offer snorkeling equipment and guided tours. Snorkeling in these clear waters allows you to see the vibrant underwater world up close without the need for extensive diving equipment or training.

The island's volcanic origin has endowed it with fertile soil, which supports a variety of agricultural activities. Taveuni is known for its organic farms and gardens, where visitors can learn about local agriculture and taste fresh tropical fruits. The island is particularly famous for its taro, a staple root crop in Fijian cuisine. Visiting a local farm provides insight into the traditional farming practices and the importance of agriculture in the local economy.

Cultural experiences on Taveuni are an integral part of any visit. The island is home to several traditional Fijian villages where you can experience the local way of life. Participating in a kava ceremony, where the traditional kava drink is shared, is a common cultural activity. This ceremony is an important social ritual in Fiji and offers a unique opportunity to connect with the local community. Villagers are welcoming and often eager to share their customs, music, and dances with visitors.

Taveuni also offers opportunities for birdwatching, as it is home to several endemic bird species. The orange dove and the silktail are two of the rare birds that can be found on the island. Birdwatching tours are available, led by knowledgeable guides who can help you spot these elusive species and provide information about their habitats and behaviors.

For a bit of history and a unique geographical experience, visit the 180th Meridian, which runs through Taveuni. This meridian marks the line of longitude that separates two calendar days. You can stand with one foot in yesterday and one foot in today, a fun and interesting photo opportunity. The meridian is marked by a sign, and there are several spots on the island where you can experience this geographical curiosity.

Accommodation on Taveuni ranges from luxury resorts to more budget-friendly lodges and guesthouses. Many of the resorts are located on the beachfront and offer stunning views of the ocean. They provide a range of amenities, including spa services, guided tours, and water sports equipment. Staying at one of these resorts allows you to enjoy the natural beauty of Taveuni while indulging in comfort and luxury. For those seeking a more rustic experience, there are several eco-lodges and budget accommodations that offer a closer connection to nature.

Food on Taveuni is a delightful blend of traditional Fijian cuisine and international flavors. Fresh seafood, tropical fruits, and root vegetables are staples in the local diet. Many resorts and restaurants on the island emphasize farm-to-table dining, using locally sourced ingredients to create delicious and healthy meals. Trying traditional dishes such as kokoda (a marinated raw fish dish) and lovo (food cooked in an underground oven) is a must for any visitor.

Exploring Taveuni also means taking the time to relax and enjoy the island's tranquil atmosphere. The slower pace of life on Taveuni allows you to unwind and connect with the natural surroundings. Whether you are lounging on a beach, swimming in a waterfall pool, or enjoying a sunset over the ocean, Taveuni provides a serene and rejuvenating environment.

Kadavu

Exploring Kadavu in Fiji offers a unique blend of untouched natural beauty, rich cultural experiences, and exceptional marine adventures. Kadavu is one of Fiji's larger islands but remains less developed and less visited compared to the more popular tourist destinations. This makes it an ideal location for travelers seeking an authentic and serene Fijian experience.

Kadavu is renowned for its pristine environment, which includes lush rainforests, rugged mountains, and stunning beaches. The island's natural beauty is largely protected, and much of its landscape remains untouched by modern development. This allows visitors to experience the island's ecosystems in their most natural state. Hiking through Kadavu's rainforests is a must-do activity. The island's dense forests are home to an array of flora and fauna, many of which are unique to the region. Walking trails wind through the forests, offering opportunities to see exotic birds, colorful butterflies, and other wildlife.

One of the most famous attractions on Kadavu is the Great Astrolabe Reef, which is the fourth-largest barrier reef in the world. This reef is a paradise for divers and snorkelers, offering some of the best underwater experiences in Fiji. The reef is teeming with marine life, including vibrant coral formations, tropical fish, manta rays, and sharks. The clear waters and excellent visibility make it a perfect spot for both beginners and experienced divers. Dive sites such as Eagle Rock and Naiqoro Passage are particularly popular, offering stunning underwater landscapes and abundant marine biodiversity. For those new to diving, there are several dive operators on the island that offer courses and guided dives.

Snorkeling in Kadavu is equally rewarding. The shallow reefs close to the shore are easily accessible and provide a colorful and diverse underwater world. Snorkeling gear can be rented from most resorts, and guided snorkeling tours are available for those who want to learn more about the marine life and coral ecosystems. The warm, clear waters make snorkeling a relaxing and enjoyable activity for visitors of all ages.

In addition to its natural beauty, Kadavu offers rich cultural experiences. The island is home to several traditional Fijian villages where you can immerse yourself in the local way of life. Visitors are often welcomed with a traditional kava ceremony, which is an important social ritual in Fiji. This ceremony involves the preparation and drinking of kava, a beverage made from the root of the kava plant. Participating in a kava ceremony is a unique opportunity to connect with the local community and learn about their customs and traditions.

Exploring Kadavu's villages also provides insight into the island's history and heritage. The villagers are known for their warmth and hospitality, and they are eager to share their culture with visitors. You can learn about traditional Fijian crafts, such as mat weaving and tapa cloth making, and even try your hand at these ancient arts. Attending a meke performance, which is a traditional Fijian dance, is another highlight. These performances are often held in the villages and involve storytelling through dance and music, providing a vibrant display of Fijian culture.

For those interested in marine conservation, Kadavu offers several opportunities to get involved. The island's community is actively engaged in protecting their natural resources, and there are various conservation projects that visitors can participate in. These include coral planting, beach clean-ups, and turtle conservation programs. Volunteering for these projects not only helps preserve Kadavu's natural beauty but also provides a deeper understanding of the island's ecosystems and the efforts being made to protect them.

Fishing is another popular activity in Kadavu. The waters around the island are rich with fish, making it an excellent spot for both recreational and sport fishing. Local guides offer fishing charters, providing all the necessary equipment and expertise to help you catch fish such as tuna, marlin, and mahi-mahi. Fishing trips can be arranged for half-day or full-day excursions, and they often include the opportunity to learn traditional Fijian fishing techniques.

Accommodation on Kadavu ranges from luxury resorts to more modest lodges and guesthouses. Many of the resorts are located on private beaches and offer stunning views of the ocean. These resorts provide a range of amenities, including spa services, gourmet dining, and various water sports. Staying at one of these resorts allows you to enjoy the natural beauty of Kadavu while indulging in comfort and luxury. For those seeking a more rustic experience, there are eco-lodges and budget accommodations that offer a closer connection to nature.

The island's cuisine is another highlight of visiting Kadavu. Fresh seafood, tropical fruits, and root vegetables are staples in the local diet. Many resorts and restaurants on the island emphasize farm-to-table dining, using locally sourced ingredients to create delicious and healthy meals. Traditional Fijian dishes such as kokoda (marinated raw fish) and lovo (food cooked in an underground oven) are must-tries. The local markets are also worth visiting, where you can find fresh produce and handmade crafts.

One of the unique aspects of exploring Kadavu is the slower pace of life. The island's tranquility and natural beauty provide a perfect escape from the hustle and bustle of everyday life. Whether you are hiking through the rainforest, diving in the clear waters, or simply relaxing on a secluded beach, Kadavu offers a serene and rejuvenating environment.

For adventure seekers, Kadavu offers plenty of activities to keep you engaged. Kayaking, paddleboarding, and sailing are popular water sports that allow you to explore the island's coastline and surrounding waters. The sheltered bays and calm lagoons provide ideal conditions for these activities. Many resorts offer equipment rental and guided tours, ensuring you have everything you need for a safe and enjoyable adventure.

Birdwatching is another activity that attracts nature enthusiasts to Kadavu. The island is home to several endemic bird species, such as the Kadavu parrot and the whistling dove. Birdwatching tours can be arranged with local guides who are knowledgeable about the best spots to see these unique birds. The island's diverse habitats, from rainforests to coastal areas, provide excellent opportunities for spotting a variety of bird species.

Lau Group

Exploring the Lau Group in Fiji is a journey into one of the most remote and culturally rich parts of the country. The Lau Group, an archipelago of about 60 islands and islets, is located in the eastern part of Fiji. These islands are less frequented by tourists, offering a unique and unspoiled experience that combines breathtaking natural beauty, rich marine life, and a deep sense of tradition and culture.

The Lau Islands are known for their stunning landscapes, which include pristine beaches, crystal-clear lagoons, and lush tropical vegetation. The natural beauty of these islands is complemented by their relative isolation, which has helped preserve their traditional way of life. This isolation makes the Lau Group an ideal destination for those seeking to escape the hustle and bustle of more tourist-heavy areas and immerse themselves in a more authentic and serene environment.

One of the most striking features of the Lau Group is its coral reefs and marine biodiversity. The waters surrounding these islands are home to some of the most vibrant and diverse coral ecosystems in the world. Snorkeling and diving in the

Lau Group provide opportunities to see a wide array of marine life, including colorful coral gardens, tropical fish, and larger species such as manta rays and sharks. The clarity of the water and the health of the coral reefs make these activities particularly rewarding. Diving spots like the reefs around Vanua Balavu and Lakeba Island are renowned for their underwater beauty.

The Lau Group is also a paradise for sailors and yachtsmen. The islands are spread out over a large area, making them perfect for island-hopping adventures. Sailing through the Lau Group allows you to explore multiple islands, each with its own unique charm and attractions. The calm lagoons and sheltered anchorages provide ideal conditions for sailing. Many sailing expeditions offer guided tours that include stops at various islands, where you can explore local villages, hike through lush landscapes, and enjoy the pristine beaches.

Cultural experiences are a highlight of visiting the Lau Group. The islands are home to traditional Fijian villages where the way of life has remained largely unchanged for centuries. Visitors are often welcomed with a traditional kava ceremony, which is an important social and cultural ritual in Fiji. Participating in a kava ceremony offers a unique opportunity to connect with the local community and learn about their customs and traditions. The villagers in the Lau Group are known for their hospitality and are eager to share their culture with visitors. You can learn about traditional Fijian crafts, such as mat weaving and tapa cloth making, and witness traditional dances and music performances.

One of the most culturally significant islands in the Lau Group is Lakeba, often considered the cultural and historical heart of the archipelago. Lakeba is known for its strong adherence to traditional customs and its role in the spread of Christianity in Fiji. The island has several historical sites, including old mission stations and churches, which provide insight into the island's history and cultural evolution. Exploring Lakeba offers a deeper understanding of the Lau Group's heritage and its importance in Fijian culture.

For nature enthusiasts, the Lau Group offers a range of outdoor activities. Hiking through the islands' interior allows you to experience the diverse flora and fauna of the region. The islands are covered in dense tropical forests, home to a variety of bird species and other wildlife. Trails lead through the forests to scenic viewpoints, waterfalls, and hidden beaches. One notable hike is on Vanua Balavu, where you can trek to the top of the island's volcanic peaks for panoramic views of the surrounding islands and ocean.

Birdwatching is another popular activity in the Lau Group. The islands are home to several endemic bird species, such as the collared lory and the silktail. Birdwatching tours can be arranged with local guides who are knowledgeable about the best spots to see these unique birds. The island's diverse habitats, from coastal areas to inland forests, provide excellent opportunities for spotting a variety of bird species.

Fishing is also a significant activity in the Lau Group. The waters around the islands are rich with fish, making it an excellent spot for both recreational and subsistence fishing. Local guides offer fishing charters, providing all the necessary equipment and expertise to help you catch fish such as tuna, marlin, and mahi-mahi. Fishing trips can be arranged for half-day or full-day excursions, and they often include the opportunity to learn traditional Fijian fishing techniques.

The Lau Group's isolation has also contributed to the preservation of its natural environment. Many of the islands are part of marine protected areas, where fishing and other activities are regulated to ensure the sustainability of the marine ecosystems. Visitors can participate in conservation projects, such as coral planting and beach clean-ups, to help preserve the natural beauty of the islands.

Accommodation in the Lau Group is more limited compared to the more developed parts of Fiji, but this adds to the charm and authenticity of the experience. Options range from small guesthouses and eco-lodges to more traditional homestays. Staying in a local village provides a unique opportunity to experience the traditional Fijian way of life and enjoy the warm hospitality of the local people. The accommodations may be basic, but they offer all the essential comforts and a close connection to nature.

The cuisine in the Lau Group reflects the island's reliance on local produce and seafood. Fresh fish, tropical fruits, and root vegetables are staples in the local diet. Traditional dishes such as kokoda (marinated raw fish) and lovo (food cooked in an underground oven) are must-tries. Many villages and guesthouses offer meals prepared with locally sourced ingredients, providing a taste of authentic Fijian cuisine.

CHAPTER 4

MUST-SEE ATTRACTIONS

Sigatoka Sand Dunes National Park

Sigatoka Sand Dunes National Park is one of Fiji's most remarkable and significant natural attractions, offering visitors a unique glimpse into the country's diverse landscapes, rich history, and cultural heritage. Located on the island of Viti Levu, near the mouth of the Sigatoka River, this national park covers an area of about 650 hectares and is renowned for its impressive sand dunes, which rise up to 60 meters high.

The Sigatoka Sand Dunes are the result of thousands of years of natural processes involving wind, rain, and the Sigatoka River. These dunes stretch along the coastline for several kilometers and offer a dramatic and ever-changing landscape that is quite different from the typical tropical scenery found elsewhere in Fiji. The dunes are a dynamic environment, with the sand constantly shifting and reshaping due to the wind, creating an otherworldly atmosphere that is both tranquil and awe-inspiring.

One of the key reasons to visit the Sigatoka Sand Dunes National Park is its geological significance. The dunes are considered one of Fiji's natural wonders, and their formation provides valuable insights into the island's geological history. The park is a living laboratory where scientists study the processes of dune formation and the impact of environmental changes on coastal ecosystems. For visitors, this means an opportunity to see a unique and fascinating landscape that is continually evolving.

The park is also a site of immense archaeological importance. Excavations at the Sigatoka Sand Dunes have unearthed artifacts that date back over 2,600 years, making it one of the most significant archaeological sites in the Pacific. These artifacts include pottery shards, tools, and human remains that provide a glimpse into the lives of Fiji's earliest inhabitants. The dunes are believed to have been inhabited by the Lapita people, who are considered the ancestors of modern Polynesians. Visiting the park offers a chance to learn about this ancient culture and see some of the artifacts that have been uncovered.

The Sigatoka Sand Dunes National Park is not just a geological and archaeological treasure; it is also a haven for biodiversity. The park is home to a variety of plant and animal species, some of which are endemic to the region. The coastal vegetation includes grasses, shrubs, and trees that have adapted to the sandy and salty environment. Birdwatchers will find the park particularly appealing, as it is home to several bird species, including the Fiji Bush Warbler and the Pacific Swallow. The diverse habitats within the park, ranging from sand dunes to forests and coastal areas, support a rich array of wildlife.

For those who enjoy outdoor activities, the Sigatoka Sand Dunes National Park offers several well-marked trails that allow visitors to explore the area at their own pace. The trails vary in length and difficulty, catering to different fitness levels and interests. One of the most popular trails is the short loop trail, which takes about an hour to complete and offers stunning views of the dunes and the coastline. For a more challenging hike, the longer trail takes about two hours and leads through the forest and along the ridges of the dunes, providing panoramic views of the surrounding landscape.

As you walk through the park, you will find interpretive signs that provide information about the natural and cultural history of the area. These signs enhance the visitor experience by explaining the significance of the dunes, the archaeological findings, and the plant and animal life that inhabit the park. Guided tours are also available and are led by knowledgeable park rangers who can provide deeper insights into the park's history and ecology.

The Sigatoka Sand Dunes National Park is also an important site for cultural heritage. The local Fijian communities have a deep connection to the land and its history. Traditional practices and stories are passed down through generations, and the park is a place where visitors can learn about Fijian customs and traditions. Participating in a guided tour with a local guide can provide a more immersive cultural experience, allowing you to understand the significance of the dunes in Fijian culture.

Conservation is a key focus of the Sigatoka Sand Dunes National Park. The park is managed by the National Trust of Fiji, which works to protect and preserve the natural and cultural heritage of the area. Efforts include reforestation projects, erosion control, and the protection of archaeological sites. Visitors can support these conservation efforts by following the park's guidelines, staying on designated trails, and participating in volunteer programs such as tree planting and beach clean-ups.

The park's visitor center provides additional resources and information for those interested in learning more about the Sigatoka Sand Dunes. The center features exhibits on the geological formation of the dunes, the archaeological discoveries, and the flora and fauna of the park. It also offers educational programs for school groups and visitors, emphasizing the importance of conservation and the preservation of cultural heritage.

Garden of the Sleeping Giant

The Garden of the Sleeping Giant is a renowned botanical garden in Fiji, located just outside of Nadi, at the foothills of the Nausori Highlands. It is one of Fiji's most enchanting attractions, celebrated for its vast collection of orchids and other tropical plants. The garden provides a serene and lush environment that offers a stark contrast to the island's more rugged and coastal landscapes.

The Garden of the Sleeping Giant was established in 1977 by the late Raymond Burr, a famous actor best known for his roles in "Perry Mason" and "Ironside." Burr was an avid orchid collector, and he created the garden to house his extensive collection. Originally intended as a private sanctuary for his orchids, the garden was later opened to the public and has since become one of Fiji's premier attractions. The name of the garden is inspired by a nearby mountain range that resembles a sleeping giant when viewed from a distance.

Spanning over 20 hectares, the garden is home to more than 2,000 different varieties of orchids, as well as a wide range of other tropical plants. As you wander through the garden, you will be greeted by vibrant displays of color and an array of exotic fragrances. The orchids are the main highlight, with species ranging from delicate, miniature orchids to large, flamboyant blooms. The garden also features collections of Asian orchids, showcasing the diversity and beauty of these remarkable flowers.

The garden is meticulously maintained, with well-marked paths and shaded walkways that guide you through the various sections. As you explore, you will come across different themed areas, each offering a unique perspective on tropical horticulture. The carefully curated landscapes include tranquil lily ponds, shady fern groves, and vibrant flower beds. Benches and resting spots are strategically placed throughout the garden, allowing visitors to sit and soak in the beauty of their surroundings.

One of the most striking features of the Garden of the Sleeping Giant is its rainforest walk. This section of the garden takes you through a dense, tropical rainforest, providing an immersive experience in Fiji's natural flora. The rainforest walk is designed to highlight the rich biodiversity of the region, with towering trees, lush undergrowth, and a variety of bird species. The cool, shaded environment of the rainforest walk offers a refreshing escape from the tropical heat, making it a favorite spot for visitors.

The garden also features a large collection of tropical fruit trees, including mango, guava, and papaya. These trees not only add to the visual appeal of the garden but also provide an opportunity to learn about the different fruits that are an integral part of Fijian cuisine. During the fruiting season, you might even have the chance to sample some of the fresh, ripe fruits directly from the trees.

Another significant aspect of the Garden of the Sleeping Giant is its focus on conservation and education. The garden serves as a living museum, dedicated to the preservation of rare and endangered plant species. Educational programs and guided tours are offered to visitors, providing insights into the importance of plant conservation and the role of botanical gardens in protecting biodiversity. Knowledgeable guides share fascinating stories about the history of the garden, the different plant species, and the efforts being made to conserve them.

The garden is also a popular venue for weddings and special events, thanks to its picturesque setting and tranquil ambiance. The beautiful surroundings provide a stunning backdrop for ceremonies and celebrations, making it a memorable location for any occasion. Events held at the garden are managed with a focus on sustainability, ensuring that the natural environment is protected and preserved.

For those who enjoy photography, the Garden of the Sleeping Giant is a paradise. The vibrant colors, diverse plant life, and stunning landscapes offer endless opportunities for capturing beautiful images. Whether you are an amateur photographer or a seasoned professional, the garden provides a wealth of inspiration and subject matter.

Visitors to the Garden of the Sleeping Giant can also enjoy a relaxing picnic in the designated picnic areas. These spots are equipped with tables and benches, allowing you to enjoy a meal surrounded by the beauty of the garden. It's a perfect way to take a break and fully immerse yourself in the tranquil environment.

The garden's visitor center offers additional resources and information for those interested in learning more about the plants and the history of the garden. The center features exhibits on the different orchid species, the history of the garden, and the life of Raymond Burr. It also provides information on the various conservation efforts being undertaken to protect the unique plant species found in the garden.

Navua River and Waterfalls

Exploring the Navua River and its waterfalls is an essential experience for anyone visiting Fiji. This captivating destination offers a blend of adventure, natural beauty, and cultural richness that makes it one of the country's most cherished attractions. Located on the main island of Viti Levu, the Navua River flows through lush rainforests and rugged terrain, creating a picturesque landscape that captivates all who visit.

The Navua River originates from the highlands of Viti Levu and winds its way through dense forests, steep gorges, and rolling hills before emptying into the Pacific Ocean. The journey along the river is marked by an ever-changing landscape, from tranquil, meandering stretches to dramatic rapids and cascading waterfalls. This diverse terrain provides a perfect setting for a variety of activities, making the Navua River a destination that caters to both adventure seekers and those looking to relax and soak in the natural beauty.

One of the primary activities that draw visitors to the Navua River is river rafting. The river's rapids offer an exhilarating experience for both novice and experienced rafters. Guided rafting tours take you through some of the most scenic parts of the river, navigating through rapids that range from gentle to challenging. As you paddle down the river, you are surrounded by the lush greenery of the rainforest, the sounds of tropical birds, and the sight of waterfalls cascading down the cliffs. The thrill of the rapids combined with the serene beauty of the surroundings makes for an unforgettable adventure.

For those who prefer a more leisurely pace, canoeing and kayaking are excellent alternatives. Paddling along the calmer sections of the river allows you to fully appreciate the tranquility and beauty of the environment. The clear, cool waters of the Navua River are perfect for a relaxing paddle, with plenty of opportunities to stop and explore along the way. Canoe tours often include visits to remote waterfalls and swimming holes, where you can take a refreshing dip in the crystal-clear waters.

The waterfalls along the Navua River are among the most stunning natural features in Fiji. These waterfalls vary in size and accessibility, with some being easily reached by boat or a short hike, while others require more effort to explore. One of the most famous waterfalls is the Navua River Waterfall, a magnificent cascade that plunges into a deep pool surrounded by lush vegetation. The sight and sound of the water crashing down into the pool create a mesmerizing experience. Swimming in the pool beneath the waterfall is a highlight for many visitors, offering a chance to cool off and enjoy the natural beauty up close.

Another notable waterfall is the Wainikoroiluva Waterfall, located deeper in the rainforest. Reaching this waterfall involves a hike through the jungle, crossing streams and navigating through the dense foliage. The journey is well worth the effort, as the waterfall itself is a breathtaking sight, with water tumbling down a series of rocky tiers into a pristine pool. The hike to Wainikoroiluva Waterfall provides an immersive experience in Fiji's tropical rainforest, allowing you to see a variety of plants and wildlife along the way.

In addition to the natural beauty, the Navua River region is rich in cultural experiences. The area is home to several traditional Fijian villages, where you can learn about the local way of life and participate in cultural activities. Visiting a village often includes a traditional kava ceremony, where you are welcomed with a drink made from the root of the kava plant. This ceremony is an important social ritual in Fijian culture and provides a unique opportunity to connect with the local community.

Village tours also offer insights into traditional Fijian crafts and practices. You can see demonstrations of mat weaving, pottery making, and tapa cloth painting, and even try your hand at these crafts. The villagers are known for their hospitality and are eager to share their culture with visitors. A typical village visit may also include a traditional Fijian meal, allowing you to taste local dishes prepared with fresh, locally sourced ingredients.

Another cultural highlight is the opportunity to witness traditional Fijian dances and music. These performances are often held in the villages and feature vibrant costumes, rhythmic drumming, and storytelling through dance. The meke, a traditional Fijian dance, is particularly captivating, with dancers moving in unison to tell stories of the island's history and legends. Watching a meke performance is a powerful and moving experience that provides a deeper understanding of Fijian culture and traditions.

For nature enthusiasts, the Navua River region offers excellent opportunities for birdwatching and wildlife spotting. The dense rainforests are home to a variety of bird species, including the colorful collared lory and the shy pink-billed parrotfinch. Birdwatching tours can be arranged with local guides who are knowledgeable about the best spots to see these unique birds. In addition to birds, the rainforest is inhabited by other wildlife such as fruit bats, lizards, and frogs, making it a rich and diverse ecosystem to explore.

The Navua River and its surrounding area are also important sites for conservation efforts. Various organizations work to protect the river's natural environment and promote sustainable tourism practices. Visitors can support these efforts by participating in conservation activities, such as river clean-ups and tree planting projects. These initiatives help preserve the pristine beauty of the Navua River and ensure that future generations can continue to enjoy this remarkable natural wonder.

Accommodation options near the Navua River range from eco-friendly lodges to more luxurious resorts. Many of these accommodations are designed to blend in with the natural surroundings, offering a peaceful and immersive experience.

Staying at one of these lodges allows you to wake up to the sounds of the rainforest, enjoy fresh local cuisine, and participate in guided tours and activities. The emphasis on sustainability and eco-tourism ensures that your visit has a positive impact on the environment and the local community.

Sri Siva Subramaniya Temple

The Sri Siva Subramaniya Temple in Nadi, Fiji, is a stunning example of Dravidian architecture and a significant cultural landmark, making it a must-see attraction for anyone visiting Fiji. This temple is the largest Hindu temple in the Southern Hemisphere, dedicated to Lord Murugan, the Hindu god of war. The temple's vibrant colors, intricate carvings, and spiritual ambiance offer a unique glimpse into Fiji's diverse cultural and religious landscape.

The Sri Siva Subramaniya Temple stands out with its impressive architecture, which reflects traditional South Indian temple design. The temple was built in the early 20th century and has undergone several renovations and expansions to maintain its grandeur. Its construction follows the Dravidian architectural style, characterized by towering gopurams (gateway towers), richly adorned with sculptures and carvings depicting various deities, mythological figures, and motifs from Hindu mythology. The temple's vibrant exterior is painted in bright colors, symbolizing the rich tapestry of Hindu beliefs and traditions.

Upon approaching the temple, visitors are greeted by the towering gopuram, which serves as the main entrance. This multi-tiered structure is adorned with intricate carvings and colorful statues of Hindu gods and goddesses. The detailed craftsmanship is a testament to the skill and devotion of the artisans who created it. The gopuram's height and elaborate design make it an iconic landmark in Nadi, visible from a distance and drawing visitors in with its striking presence.

Entering the temple complex, you are immediately enveloped in a sense of peace and spirituality. The temple grounds are meticulously maintained, with beautifully landscaped gardens and pathways leading to the various shrines and prayer halls. The main shrine is dedicated to Lord Murugan, also known as Kartikeya or Subramanya, who is revered as a protector and warrior. Inside the sanctum, a magnificent statue of Lord Murugan stands, adorned with traditional decorations and offerings from devotees. The statue's serene expression and intricate details convey a sense of divine presence, inviting worshippers and visitors to reflect and connect with the spiritual energy of the temple.

In addition to the main shrine, the temple complex houses several other shrines dedicated to various deities, including Lord Ganesha, the elephant-headed god of wisdom and new beginnings, and Lord Shiva, the destroyer and transformer. Each shrine is uniquely decorated and offers a place for devotees to perform rituals and offer prayers. The temple's layout and design are carefully planned to facilitate the movement of worshippers and create a harmonious flow of energy throughout the complex.

The temple is not only a place of worship but also a center for cultural and religious activities. Throughout the year, the Sri Siva Subramaniya Temple hosts numerous festivals and events that attract devotees and tourists alike. One of the most significant festivals celebrated at the temple is Thaipusam, a Hindu festival dedicated to Lord Murugan. During Thaipusam, devotees engage in various acts of devotion, including carrying kavadis (ornate structures) and participating in elaborate processions. The festival is marked by vibrant colors, traditional music, and dance performances, creating a lively and spiritually charged atmosphere.

Another important festival celebrated at the temple is the Tamil New Year, known as Puthandu. This festival marks the beginning of the Tamil calendar year and is celebrated with special prayers, rituals, and feasts. Visiting the temple during these festivals provides a unique opportunity to witness and participate in traditional Hindu practices and experience the rich cultural heritage of Fiji's Indian community.

The Sri Siva Subramaniya Temple also plays a vital role in the local community by offering educational and social services. The temple conducts religious classes, cultural programs, and workshops to educate the younger generation about Hindu traditions and values. These programs help preserve and promote the cultural identity of the Indian community in Fiji. Additionally, the temple is involved in various charitable activities, providing support and assistance to those in need.

For visitors interested in learning more about Hinduism and the temple's history, guided tours are available. Knowledgeable guides provide insights into the significance of the various deities, the symbolism behind the temple's architecture, and the rituals and customs practiced by devotees. These tours offer a deeper understanding of the temple's spiritual and cultural importance, enhancing the overall visitor experience.

The serene and tranquil environment of the Sri Siva Subramaniya Temple makes it an ideal place for meditation and reflection. Many visitors come to the temple to seek solace and find inner peace amidst the bustling surroundings of Nadi. The temple's peaceful ambiance, combined with the sounds of devotional music and the fragrance of incense, creates a perfect setting for spiritual contemplation and rejuvenation.

The temple is open to visitors of all faiths, and everyone is welcome to explore and experience its beauty and serenity. It is important to observe the temple's guidelines and dress modestly when visiting. Shoes should be removed before entering the temple complex, and respectful behavior should be maintained at all times. Photography is allowed in certain areas, but it is advisable to seek permission before taking pictures of the shrines and statues.

Fiji Museum

The Fiji Museum, located in Suva's Thurston Gardens, is an essential destination for anyone visiting Fiji. As one of the oldest and most comprehensive museums in the South Pacific, it provides an in-depth look into the rich cultural heritage, history, and natural environment of Fiji.

The Fiji Museum was established in 1904 and has since become a repository of the nation's history and culture. It houses an extensive collection of artifacts that span over 3,700 years, offering a comprehensive overview of Fiji's past and its development over millennia. The museum's exhibits are meticulously curated to provide insights into the lives, traditions, and achievements of the Fijian people, from the early Lapita settlers to the modern multicultural society of today.

Upon entering the museum, visitors are immediately drawn into a journey through time. The galleries are arranged to lead you chronologically through Fiji's history, starting with the ancient Lapita culture. The Lapita people, who are believed to be the ancestors of the Polynesians, were the first settlers in Fiji. The museum's collection includes pottery shards, tools, and other artifacts that provide a glimpse into the life and craftsmanship of these early inhabitants. The distinctive pottery, decorated with intricate geometric patterns, is particularly noteworthy and is considered one of the hallmarks of Lapita culture.

The museum also showcases the cultural and social developments of the Fijian people. Exhibits on traditional Fijian society include a wide range of artifacts such as weapons, fishing gear, and domestic utensils. These items highlight the ingenuity and skills of the Fijian people in their daily lives and survival in a challenging environment. One of the most striking displays is the collection of war clubs and spears, which were used in traditional Fijian warfare. These weapons are not only functional but also intricately carved and decorated, reflecting the artistry and craftsmanship of their makers.

A significant part of the museum's collection is dedicated to Fijian seafaring and navigation. The Fijians were skilled sailors and navigators, and their knowledge of the ocean and its currents allowed them to travel vast distances. The museum features traditional double-hulled canoes, known as drua, which were used for long voyages and inter-island travel. These canoes are remarkable for their size and construction, and the exhibit provides detailed information on the techniques used to build and navigate them.

The museum also explores the impact of European contact on Fijian society. The arrival of European explorers, missionaries, and traders in the 18th and 19th centuries brought significant changes to Fiji. Exhibits on this period include artifacts such as tools, clothing, and personal items belonging to early European settlers, as well as items that illustrate the interactions between Europeans and Fijians. This section of the museum provides a nuanced view of the cultural exchanges, conflicts, and transformations that occurred during this time.

One of the most poignant exhibits in the museum is dedicated to the indentured labor system. In the late 19th and early 20th centuries, thousands of Indians were brought to Fiji to work on sugarcane plantations under the indenture system. The museum's collection includes personal items, documents, and photographs that tell the stories of these laborers and their contributions to Fijian society. This exhibit offers a moving and informative perspective on the hardships and resilience of the indentured laborers and their lasting impact on Fiji's multicultural landscape.

In addition to its historical exhibits, the Fiji Museum also features sections dedicated to the natural environment of Fiji. The museum's natural history collection includes specimens of Fiji's unique flora and fauna, providing insights into the island's biodiversity. Displays on Fiji's marine life, birds, and plant species highlight the richness of the natural environment and the importance of conservation efforts to protect these resources.

The Fiji Museum is not just a place to view artifacts; it is also a center for research and education. The museum conducts research on various aspects of Fijian culture, history, and natural heritage, contributing to the preservation and understanding of Fiji's heritage. Educational programs and workshops are offered to school groups and visitors, providing hands-on learning experiences and fostering a deeper appreciation of Fijian culture. The museum also hosts temporary exhibitions and cultural events, showcasing contemporary Fijian art and culture.

The museum's location in Thurston Gardens adds to its appeal. Thurston Gardens, named after a former governor of Fiji, is a beautiful botanical garden that features a wide variety of tropical plants and trees. Visitors to the museum can enjoy a stroll through the gardens, which provide a peaceful and scenic setting. The gardens are also home to several other historical landmarks, including the Old Town Hall and the Clock Tower, adding to the historical and cultural significance of the area.

For those interested in archaeology, the museum offers a fascinating look at the ongoing efforts to uncover and preserve Fiji's ancient past. The museum collaborates with archaeologists and researchers to excavate and study sites across Fiji, and some of the findings are displayed in the museum. This provides visitors with a glimpse into the process of archaeological discovery and the continuous efforts to learn more about Fiji's early history.

The museum's gift shop offers a range of souvenirs, books, and crafts that reflect Fijian culture and heritage. Purchasing items from the gift shop supports the museum's efforts to preserve and promote Fijian history and culture. The shop features handmade items by local artisans, providing an opportunity to take home a piece of Fiji's artistic traditions.

Colo-I-Suva Forest Park

Colo-I-Suva Forest Park, located on the island of Viti Levu, is one of Fiji's most captivating natural attractions. This lush rainforest park, just a short drive from the capital city of Suva, offers visitors an opportunity to immerse themselves in the natural beauty of Fiji. With its diverse flora and fauna, serene swimming holes, and numerous hiking trails, Colo-I-Suva Forest Park provides a tranquil escape from the hustle and bustle of urban life.

The park covers an area of approximately 2.5 square kilometers and is renowned for its dense rainforest, which is home to a wide variety of plant and animal species. As you enter the park, you are greeted by towering trees, thick underbrush, and the sounds of birds and other wildlife. The forest is a testament to Fiji's rich natural heritage, offering a pristine environment that has been carefully preserved.

One of the main attractions of Colo-I-Suva Forest Park is its extensive network of hiking trails. These trails range from easy walks to more challenging hikes, catering to visitors of all fitness levels. The trails are well-marked and maintained, winding through the rainforest and offering stunning views of the natural surroundings. As you hike, you will encounter a variety of native plants and trees, some of which are unique to Fiji. The lush vegetation creates a cool, shaded environment, making the hikes comfortable even during the hotter parts of the day.

The park's trails also lead to several natural swimming holes and waterfalls, which are perfect for a refreshing dip. One of the most popular spots is the Waisila Creek, where you can swim in clear, cool water surrounded by the beauty of the rainforest. The natural pools vary in size and depth, providing options for both swimmers and those who prefer to wade in the shallower areas. The waterfalls cascading into these pools add to the scenic beauty, creating a serene and picturesque setting.

Birdwatching is another popular activity in Colo-I-Suva Forest Park. The park is home to numerous bird species, making it a haven for bird enthusiasts. Some of the birds you might spot include the colorful collared lory, the Fiji bush warbler, and the pink-billed parrotfinch. The dense forest provides ample opportunities for birdwatching, with many birds nesting and feeding in the canopy above. Bringing a pair of binoculars and a bird guide can enhance your experience, allowing you to identify and appreciate the diverse avian life.

Colo-I-Suva Forest Park is also an important site for conservation. The park plays a crucial role in protecting the region's biodiversity and preserving its natural habitats. Efforts to conserve the park's flora and fauna include reforestation projects, invasive species control, and habitat restoration. Visitors to the park can support these efforts by following the park's guidelines, such as staying on designated trails, not disturbing wildlife, and taking any litter with them. Educational programs and guided tours are available, providing insights into the park's conservation initiatives and the importance of protecting natural ecosystems.

For those interested in the cultural aspects of the park, Colo-I-Suva offers a glimpse into the traditional uses of the forest by indigenous Fijians. Many of the plants found in the park have been used for centuries for medicinal purposes, food, and building materials. Guided tours often include information on these traditional practices, offering a deeper understanding of the relationship between the local people and their environment. Learning about the cultural significance of the forest adds an enriching dimension to the visit, highlighting the importance of preserving both natural and cultural heritage.

Picnicking is a popular activity in Colo-I-Suva Forest Park, with several designated picnic areas equipped with tables and benches. These areas provide a perfect spot to relax and enjoy a meal amidst the natural beauty of the forest. The sound of the nearby creek and the rustling of leaves in the breeze create a peaceful ambiance, making it an ideal setting for a family outing or a quiet retreat. Packing a picnic and spending the day in the park allows you to fully immerse yourself in the tranquil environment and appreciate the serenity of the forest.

Photography enthusiasts will find Colo-I-Suva Forest Park to be a treasure trove of opportunities. The park's diverse landscapes, from dense rainforest and clear swimming holes to cascading waterfalls and vibrant birdlife, provide a wide range of subjects to capture. The changing light throughout the day offers different perspectives and moods, making it a rewarding experience for photographers of all levels. Whether you are interested in landscape photography, wildlife photography, or macro photography, the park offers a wealth of inspiration.

The park's visitor center provides additional resources and information for those interested in learning more about Colo-I-Suva Forest Park. The center features exhibits on the park's history, flora and fauna, and conservation efforts. It also offers maps, trail guides, and other materials to help visitors make the most of their visit. The knowledgeable staff at the visitor center can answer questions and provide recommendations on the best trails and activities based on your interests and fitness level.

Bouma National Heritage Park

Bouma National Heritage Park, located on the island of Taveuni in Fiji, is a prime example of the country's stunning natural beauty and rich biodiversity. This expansive park covers an area of over 150 square kilometers and is renowned for its lush rainforests, cascading waterfalls, and vibrant ecosystems. It is a destination that offers a deep connection to nature, making it a must-see attraction for anyone visiting Fiji.

Bouma National Heritage Park was established in 1990 with the aim of preserving the natural and cultural heritage of the region. The park is managed by the local communities, who work together to protect its diverse ecosystems and promote sustainable tourism. This collaborative approach ensures that visitors can enjoy the park's beauty while contributing to its conservation.

One of the most striking features of Bouma National Heritage Park is its dense rainforest. The park's rainforests are home to a variety of plant and animal species, many of which are endemic to Fiji. As you explore the park, you will be surrounded by towering trees, thick undergrowth, and a symphony of sounds from birds and other wildlife. The lush vegetation creates a cool and shaded environment, providing a refreshing escape from the tropical heat.

The park is perhaps best known for its spectacular waterfalls. The Tavoro Waterfalls, a series of three falls, are one of the main attractions within the park. The first waterfall, easily accessible from the entrance, is a stunning cascade that plunges into a large pool, perfect for swimming. The clear, cool waters provide a refreshing respite after a hike through the rainforest. A well-marked trail leads to the second and third waterfalls, which are more secluded and offer a serene setting for those willing to venture further. The trail to these waterfalls takes you deeper into the forest, providing opportunities to see more of the park's diverse flora and fauna.

Hiking is a major activity in Bouma National Heritage Park, with several trails catering to different levels of fitness and interest. The Lavena Coastal Walk is one of the most popular hikes, offering a mix of coastal and jungle scenery. This trail takes you along the coast, through traditional Fijian villages, and into the rainforest, ending at a beautiful waterfall and natural swimming pool. The hike is relatively easy and can be enjoyed by visitors of all ages. Along the way, you can enjoy stunning views of the ocean, see traditional thatched bures (houses), and learn about the local way of life.

For those seeking more challenging hikes, the Vidawa Rainforest Hike offers an immersive experience in the heart of the rainforest. This guided hike takes you through dense jungle, across streams, and up to high ridges with panoramic views of Taveuni and the surrounding islands. The hike also provides insights into traditional Fijian land use and forest management practices, as your guide will share stories and knowledge about the plants and animals you encounter. The Vidawa Rainforest Hike is an excellent way to experience the raw beauty of Bouma National Heritage Park and gain a deeper appreciation for the natural world.

Birdwatching is another popular activity in Bouma National Heritage Park. The park is home to several endemic bird species, making it a haven for bird enthusiasts. Some of the birds you might spot include the silktail, the orange dove, and the red shining parrot. Birdwatching tours can be arranged with local guides who are knowledgeable about the best spots to see these unique birds. The diverse habitats within the park, from coastal areas to inland forests, provide excellent opportunities for spotting a variety of bird species.

In addition to its natural beauty, Bouma National Heritage Park is rich in cultural heritage. The park encompasses several traditional Fijian villages, where you can learn about the local way of life and participate in cultural activities. Visiting a village often includes a traditional kava ceremony, where you are welcomed with a drink made from the root of the kava plant. This ceremony is an important social ritual in Fijian culture and provides a unique opportunity to connect with the local community.

Village tours also offer insights into traditional Fijian crafts and practices. You can see demonstrations of mat weaving, tapa cloth making, and basket weaving, and even try your hand at these crafts. The villagers are known for their hospitality and are eager to share their culture with visitors. A typical village visit may also include a traditional Fijian meal, allowing you to taste local dishes prepared with fresh, locally sourced ingredients.

Bouma National Heritage Park is also an important site for conservation. The park plays a crucial role in protecting the region's biodiversity and preserving its natural habitats. Efforts to conserve the park's flora and fauna include reforestation projects, invasive species control, and habitat restoration. Visitors to the park can support these efforts by following the park's guidelines, such as staying on designated trails, not disturbing wildlife, and taking any litter with them. Educational programs and guided tours are available, providing insights into the park's conservation initiatives and the importance of protecting natural ecosystems.

The park's visitor center provides additional resources and information for those interested in learning more about Bouma National Heritage Park. The center features exhibits on the park's history, flora and fauna, and conservation efforts. It also offers maps, trail guides, and other materials to help visitors make the most of their visit. The knowledgeable staff at the visitor center can answer questions and provide recommendations on the best trails and activities based on your interests and fitness level.

Photography enthusiasts will find Bouma National Heritage Park to be a treasure trove of opportunities. The park's diverse landscapes, from dense rainforest and clear swimming holes to cascading waterfalls and vibrant birdlife, provide a wide range of subjects to capture. The changing light throughout the day offers different perspectives and moods, making it a rewarding experience for photographers of all levels. Whether you are interested in landscape photography, wildlife photography, or macro photography, the park offers a wealth of inspiration.

Picnicking is a popular activity in Bouma National Heritage Park, with several designated picnic areas equipped with tables and benches. These areas provide a perfect spot to relax and enjoy a meal amidst the natural beauty of the forest. The sound of the nearby creek and the rustling of leaves in the breeze create a peaceful ambiance, making it an ideal setting for a family outing or a quiet retreat. Packing a picnic and spending the day in the park allows you to fully immerse yourself in the tranquil environment and appreciate the serenity of the forest.

Nadi's Handicraft Market

Nadi's Handicraft Market is an essential stop for anyone visiting Fiji. Located in the heart of Nadi town, this vibrant market offers a rich array of traditional Fijian arts and crafts, making it a perfect destination for those looking to experience the local culture and bring home unique souvenirs.

The market is easily accessible and is a lively hub where locals and tourists mingle. Upon entering the market, you are greeted by a colorful array of stalls, each brimming with handmade items that reflect the rich cultural heritage of Fiji. The atmosphere is bustling, with the sounds of vendors calling out to passersby, the chatter of shoppers, and the rhythmic beats of Fijian music playing in the background. The market is a sensory feast, filled with vibrant colors, intricate textures, and enticing scents.

One of the primary attractions of Nadi's Handicraft Market is its wide selection of traditional Fijian crafts. These items are not only beautiful but also carry deep cultural significance. The market offers a variety of handcrafted goods, including masi (tapa cloth), woven baskets, wooden carvings, jewelry, and pottery. Each piece is meticulously crafted by local artisans, using techniques that have been passed down through generations. Buying these items supports the local economy and helps preserve these traditional crafts.

Masi, or tapa cloth, is one of the most iconic items available at the market. Made from the bark of the mulberry tree, masi is decorated with intricate patterns and designs that often tell stories or represent aspects of Fijian culture. The process of making masi is labor-intensive, involving several stages of soaking, pounding, and painting. The finished product is used for a variety of purposes, including clothing, ceremonial items, and wall hangings. At the market, you can find masi in various forms, from large ceremonial pieces to smaller souvenirs like bookmarks and coasters.

Woven baskets and mats are another popular item at the market. These items are made from pandanus leaves or coconut fibers and are prized for their durability and beauty. The weaving process requires great skill and patience, with artisans creating intricate patterns that are both functional and decorative. These baskets and mats are used in everyday life in Fiji, but they also make excellent souvenirs that showcase the craftsmanship of Fijian weavers.

Wooden carvings are a highlight of Nadi's Handicraft Market. Fijian woodcarving is a highly respected art form, with artisans creating detailed sculptures and household items from native hardwoods like mahogany and vesi. The carvings often depict traditional Fijian motifs, such as tiki figures, canoes, and animals. These pieces are not only decorative but also hold cultural and spiritual significance. Larger carvings, such as masks and statues, can be found alongside smaller items like bowls, utensils, and jewelry boxes. Each piece is unique, reflecting the individual style and skill of the artisan who created it.

Jewelry at the market includes items made from natural materials such as shells, pearls, and coconut shell. These pieces are crafted into necklaces, bracelets, earrings, and rings, often incorporating traditional Fijian designs. The jewelry is both beautiful and affordable, making it a popular choice for visitors looking to bring home a piece of Fiji's natural beauty.

Pottery is another traditional craft represented at the market. Fijian pottery is typically made using ancient techniques that involve hand-building and open-fire kilns. The designs are simple yet elegant, with functional items like bowls, pots, and vases available for purchase. These pieces are not only practical but also serve as a tangible connection to Fiji's cultural heritage.

The market is also a great place to find traditional Fijian clothing and textiles. Bula shirts and dresses, made from brightly colored fabrics with floral or island-inspired prints, are a popular choice. These garments are comfortable and stylish, making them perfect for the tropical climate of Fiji. You can also find sarongs, scarves, and other textile items that showcase the vibrant patterns and colors of Fijian fashion.

In addition to the crafts, the market offers a variety of other items that reflect Fijian culture. Spices, herbal medicines, and natural beauty products made from local ingredients are available, providing a glimpse into traditional Fijian remedies and wellness practices. These products are made using natural ingredients like coconut oil, turmeric, and ginger, which are known for their healing properties.

Visiting Nadi's Handicraft Market is not just about shopping; it's also an opportunity to learn about Fijian culture and history. The vendors are usually very knowledgeable about their products and are happy to share the stories behind them. Engaging with the artisans and vendors provides a deeper understanding of the significance of these crafts and the role they play in Fijian society. Many of the items you find at the market are made using traditional methods that have been preserved for centuries, making them not just souvenirs, but pieces of living history.

The market also hosts cultural performances and demonstrations, where you can see artisans at work and watch traditional Fijian dances and music. These performances add to the vibrant atmosphere of the market and provide an immersive cultural experience. Watching a traditional meke dance or listening to the harmonious sounds of Fijian music enhances your appreciation of the culture and makes your visit to the market even more memorable.

For those who enjoy haggling, the market provides an opportunity to engage in friendly negotiations with the vendors. Bargaining is a common practice at the market, and it can be a fun way to interact with the locals and potentially get a better deal on your purchases. Remember to be respectful and fair in your negotiations, as the prices reflect the hard work and skill of the artisans.

Nadi's Handicraft Market is also conveniently located near other attractions in Nadi, making it easy to incorporate a visit into your itinerary. After exploring the market, you can visit nearby sites such as the Sri Siva Subramaniya Temple, the Garden of the Sleeping Giant, or the Sabeto Hot Springs. The central location of the market makes it an ideal starting point for a day of exploration in Nadi.

CHAPTER 5

ACTIVITIES FOR EVERY TRAVELER

Activities for Solo Travelers

Fiji is an ideal destination for solo travelers, offering a rich tapestry of experiences that cater to a variety of interests and preferences. Whether you're seeking adventure, relaxation, cultural immersion, or natural beauty, Fiji has something for everyone.

One of the most enticing aspects of traveling solo in Fiji is the opportunity to explore its stunning natural landscapes. The islands boast a wealth of outdoor activities that allow you to connect with nature and experience the beauty of the South Pacific. Hiking through Fiji's lush rainforests is a must for any nature enthusiast. Trails such as those in the Colo-I-Suva Forest Park or the Bouma National Heritage Park on Taveuni offer a chance to see towering trees, vibrant birdlife, and picturesque waterfalls. These hikes vary in difficulty, catering to both casual walkers and experienced hikers. Along the way, you can take a refreshing dip in natural pools or simply enjoy the tranquility of the forest.

For those who love the ocean, Fiji's clear, warm waters are perfect for snorkeling and diving. The coral reefs surrounding the islands are teeming with marine life, including colorful fish, sea turtles, and even sharks. Popular snorkeling spots like the Coral Coast and the Mamanuca Islands provide easy access to vibrant reefs just off the shore. Diving enthusiasts can explore world-renowned sites such as the Great White Wall in the Somosomo Strait or the Rainbow Reef. These underwater adventures offer a unique glimpse into the rich biodiversity of Fiji's marine ecosystems. Many dive shops and resorts offer courses for beginners, ensuring that even those new to diving can experience the underwater wonders of Fiji.

Kayaking and paddleboarding are other excellent ways to explore Fiji's coastal beauty. Paddling along the calm lagoons and mangrove forests allows you to see the islands from a different perspective. The Yasawa Islands and the southern coast of Viti Levu are popular areas for these activities. Kayaking tours often include stops at secluded beaches and hidden coves, providing a serene and intimate experience with nature.

For solo travelers interested in cultural experiences, Fiji offers a wealth of opportunities to connect with the local way of life. Visiting traditional Fijian villages provides a deeper understanding of the island's rich heritage and customs. Many villages welcome visitors with a traditional kava ceremony, a ritual that involves drinking a beverage made from the kava root. This ceremony is an important part of Fijian culture and offers a unique opportunity to engage with the local community. Village tours often include demonstrations of traditional crafts such as mat weaving, tapa cloth making, and basket weaving. Participating in these activities allows you to learn directly from the artisans and gain a deeper appreciation for their skills and traditions.

Attending a meke performance is another way to experience Fijian culture. Meke is a traditional dance that tells stories through song and movement. These performances are often accompanied by rhythmic drumming and chanting, creating a captivating and immersive experience. Many resorts and cultural centers offer meke shows, allowing you to witness this vibrant aspect of Fijian culture firsthand.

Fiji is also known for its rich culinary traditions, and solo travelers can enjoy exploring the local food scene. Fijian cuisine is a blend of indigenous flavors and influences from Indian, Chinese, and European cuisines. Local markets such as the Suva Municipal Market or the Nadi Market are great places to sample fresh produce, seafood, and traditional dishes. Street food stalls and local eateries offer a range of delicious options, from fresh coconut water and tropical fruits to curries and seafood specialties. Trying traditional dishes like kokoda (a marinated raw fish dish) and lovo (food cooked in an underground oven) is a must for any food lover.

For those seeking relaxation and rejuvenation, Fiji's numerous spas and wellness centers provide the perfect escape. Many resorts offer spa treatments that incorporate traditional Fijian techniques and natural ingredients. A massage with coconut oil or a body scrub with local herbs can be a soothing way to unwind after a day of exploration. Yoga and meditation classes are also available at many resorts, often held in scenic outdoor settings overlooking the ocean. These wellness activities provide a chance to relax and recharge in a tranquil environment.

Exploring Fiji's history and heritage is another rewarding activity for solo travelers. The Fiji Museum in Suva offers a comprehensive overview of the island's past, with exhibits on the Lapita culture, the arrival of Europeans, and the development of modern Fiji. The museum's collection includes ancient artifacts, traditional Fijian tools, and items from the colonial era. A visit to the museum provides valuable insights into the cultural and historical context of Fiji.

For those interested in adventure sports, Fiji offers a range of thrilling activities. Zip-lining through the rainforest, skydiving over the islands, and white-water rafting on the Navua River are just a few of the options available. These activities provide an adrenaline rush and the chance to see Fiji's landscapes from a different perspective. The Yasawa Islands are known for their excellent conditions for windsurfing and kitesurfing, attracting enthusiasts from around the world.

Island hopping is another popular activity for solo travelers in Fiji. With over 300 islands to explore, each offering its unique charm, island hopping allows you to experience the diversity of Fiji. The Mamanuca and Yasawa Islands are particularly popular for their stunning beaches and clear waters. Day trips and multi-day tours are available, providing opportunities to snorkel, hike, and relax on some of Fiji's most beautiful islands.

Solo travelers can also take advantage of Fiji's vibrant nightlife. Nadi and Suva are known for their lively bars, clubs, and restaurants, offering a chance to socialize and meet fellow travelers. Many resorts also host evening entertainment, including live music, traditional dance performances, and themed parties.

Romantic Escapes for Couples

Fiji is renowned for its stunning natural beauty, warm hospitality, and idyllic settings, making it a perfect destination for couples seeking a romantic escape. Whether you're looking for luxurious resorts, secluded beaches, or adventurous activities, Fiji offers a myriad of options that cater to all types of romantic getaways.

Fiji's islands are the epitome of paradise, with their crystal-clear waters, white sandy beaches, and lush tropical landscapes. The serene and tranquil environment creates an intimate atmosphere that is perfect for couples looking to spend quality time together. One of the most appealing aspects of a romantic escape in Fiji is the opportunity to stay in a luxurious beachfront resort. Many of these resorts offer private villas or bungalows, known as bures, which are often situated right on the beach or over the water. These accommodations provide stunning views, complete privacy, and direct access to the beach, allowing couples to enjoy the beauty of Fiji from the comfort of their own space.

A stay in one of these bures often comes with a range of amenities designed to enhance the romantic experience. Private plunge pools, outdoor showers, and spacious decks with loungers and hammocks are common features. Many resorts also offer personalized services such as butlers, private chefs, and in-room spa treatments. Imagine waking up to the sound of the ocean waves, enjoying a leisurely breakfast on your private deck, and then spending the day lounging by your pool or exploring the nearby reefs.

Fiji's natural beauty provides the perfect backdrop for a variety of romantic activities. Couples can take a leisurely stroll along the pristine beaches, hand in hand, as the sun sets over the horizon. The sunsets in Fiji are particularly spectacular, with the sky painted in hues of orange, pink, and purple, creating a magical atmosphere. For a truly unforgettable experience, consider a sunset cruise. These cruises often include a gourmet dinner and champagne, allowing you to enjoy the stunning views while savoring delicious food and drink.

Snorkeling and diving are among the most popular activities in Fiji, thanks to the abundant marine life and vibrant coral reefs. Exploring the underwater world together can be a thrilling and bonding experience. The Mamanuca and Yasawa Islands are known for their excellent snorkeling and diving spots, where you can see everything from colorful fish and sea turtles to majestic manta rays and reef sharks. Many resorts offer guided snorkeling and diving tours, providing all the necessary equipment and instruction.

For those seeking a bit of adventure, kayaking and paddleboarding are great ways to explore the coastal waters. Paddling together in a double kayak or side by side on paddleboards allows you to discover hidden coves, mangrove forests, and secluded beaches. The calm, clear waters of Fiji's lagoons make these activities accessible even for beginners.

A visit to one of Fiji's many waterfalls can also be a romantic outing. Taveuni, known as the "Garden Island," is home to several beautiful waterfalls, including the Tavoro Waterfalls in Bouma National Heritage Park. These waterfalls are set in lush rainforest surroundings and offer refreshing natural pools where you can swim together. The hike to the waterfalls is scenic and relatively easy, making it a pleasant way to spend a day in nature.

Couples looking for relaxation and pampering will find plenty of options in Fiji's spas and wellness centers. Many resorts have on-site spas that offer a range of treatments, from traditional Fijian massages using coconut oil to luxurious facials and body wraps. Couples can enjoy side-by-side massages in a private cabana overlooking the ocean, creating a serene and rejuvenating experience. Yoga and meditation classes are also available at many resorts, often held in scenic outdoor settings that enhance the sense of peace and tranquility.

Dining in Fiji can be a deeply romantic experience, with many resorts offering private dining options that allow you to enjoy a meal in a secluded and intimate setting. Private beach dinners, where a table is set up on the sand with torches and candles, are particularly popular. You can enjoy a gourmet meal under the stars, with the sound of the waves providing a soothing backdrop. Some resorts also offer dining experiences in unique locations, such as a treetop platform or a secluded garden, adding an extra touch of magic to your evening.

Exploring Fiji's culture together can also be a meaningful and enriching experience. Visiting a traditional Fijian village allows you to learn about the local way of life and participate in cultural activities. Many village tours include a kava ceremony, a traditional ritual that involves drinking a beverage made from the kava root. This ceremony is an important part of Fijian culture and provides a unique opportunity to connect with the local community. Watching a traditional meke dance performance, with its rhythmic drumming and storytelling, is another cultural highlight that can be enjoyed together.

Fiji is also known for its vibrant arts and crafts scene. Visiting local markets and craft shops allows you to see and purchase handmade items such as masi (tapa cloth), woven baskets, and wooden carvings. These items make unique and meaningful souvenirs that can remind you of your romantic getaway. Engaging with local artisans and learning about their craft can also be a rewarding experience.

For those looking to explore Fiji's natural beauty further, a day trip to one of the many uninhabited islands is a must. These islands offer pristine beaches and crystal-clear waters, providing the perfect setting for a romantic picnic or a day of relaxation. Many resorts offer boat trips to these islands, complete with a packed picnic lunch and all the necessary equipment for snorkeling and swimming.

Another unforgettable experience for couples is a helicopter or seaplane tour. These tours provide a bird's-eye view of Fiji's stunning landscapes, from the coral reefs and turquoise waters to the lush rainforests and volcanic mountains. Seeing the islands from above is a breathtaking experience that adds a touch of adventure and excitement to your romantic escape.

Fun for Families with Kids

Fiji is an outstanding destination for families with kids, offering a wide array of activities and experiences that cater to all ages. The islands' natural beauty, warm hospitality, and rich culture make it a fantastic place for family vacations. From beach fun and water activities to educational excursions and cultural experiences, Fiji has something to keep every family member entertained and engaged.

Fiji's beaches are among the best in the world, providing endless opportunities for fun and relaxation. Families can spend their days building sandcastles, playing beach volleyball, or simply lounging on the soft, white sand. The calm, shallow waters of many beaches are perfect for young children to splash around in safely. Resorts often provide beach toys and equipment, making it easy for families to enjoy a day by the sea.

Snorkeling is a fantastic activity for families with kids, allowing them to explore the vibrant underwater world of Fiji's coral reefs. The clear, warm waters are teeming with colorful fish, sea turtles, and other marine life. Many resorts offer guided snorkeling tours that cater to beginners, providing all the necessary equipment and instruction. Locations such as the Coral Coast, the Mamanuca Islands, and the Yasawa Islands are known for their excellent snorkeling conditions. The shallow reefs close to shore make it easy for kids to participate and enjoy the experience.

For families with older kids or teenagers, scuba diving can be an exciting adventure. Fiji is home to some of the best dive sites in the world, including the Great White Wall and the Rainbow Reef. Dive shops and resorts offer courses for beginners, ensuring that even those new to diving can explore the underwater wonders of Fiji. Many dive operators provide family-friendly dive packages, allowing parents and children to dive together and share the experience.

Kayaking and paddleboarding are other popular water activities that are suitable for families. Paddling along the coast or through mangrove forests provides a unique perspective of the islands and allows families to explore hidden coves and secluded beaches. Double kayaks are available, making it easy for parents to paddle with younger children. Paddleboarding is a fun way for older kids to test their balance and coordination while enjoying the beautiful scenery.

A visit to one of Fiji's many waterfalls can be a memorable family outing. Taveuni, known as the "Garden Island," is home to the spectacular Tavoro Waterfalls in Bouma National Heritage Park. These waterfalls are set in lush rainforest surroundings and offer refreshing natural pools where families can swim and play. The hike to the waterfalls is scenic and relatively easy, making it suitable for kids of all ages. The park also provides picnic areas, allowing families to enjoy a meal amidst the natural beauty of the forest.

Fiji's rich culture and traditions provide numerous opportunities for educational and cultural experiences. Visiting a traditional Fijian village can be a highlight of any family vacation. Many villages welcome visitors with a traditional kava ceremony, a ritual that involves drinking a beverage made from the kava root. This ceremony is an important part of Fijian culture and provides a unique opportunity to connect with the local community. Village tours often include demonstrations of traditional crafts such as mat weaving, tapa cloth making, and basket weaving. These activities allow children to learn about Fijian culture and traditions in an interactive and engaging way.

Attending a meke performance is another way to experience Fijian culture. Meke is a traditional dance that tells stories through song and movement. These performances are often accompanied by rhythmic drumming and chanting, creating a captivating and immersive experience. Many resorts and cultural centers offer meke shows, allowing families to witness this vibrant aspect of Fijian culture firsthand.

Fiji is also known for its vibrant arts and crafts scene. Visiting local markets and craft shops allows families to see and purchase handmade items such as masi (tapa cloth), woven baskets, and wooden carvings. These items make unique and meaningful souvenirs that can remind families of their trip to Fiji. Engaging with local artisans and learning about their craft can also be a rewarding experience for children.

For families interested in history and nature, a visit to the Fiji Museum in Suva is a must. The museum offers a comprehensive overview of the island's past, with exhibits on the Lapita culture, the arrival of Europeans, and the development of modern Fiji. The museum's collection includes ancient artifacts, traditional Fijian tools, and items from the colonial era. A visit to the museum provides valuable insights into the cultural and historical context of Fiji and can be an educational experience for children.

Many resorts in Fiji offer kids' clubs and family-friendly activities, ensuring that children are entertained and parents can relax. Kids' clubs provide a range of supervised activities, including arts and crafts, games, and educational programs. These clubs are staffed by trained professionals who ensure that children are safe and engaged. Family-friendly resorts also offer amenities such as swimming pools, playgrounds, and babysitting services, making it easy for families to enjoy their stay.

For families seeking adventure, Fiji offers a range of thrilling activities. Zip-lining through the rainforest, skydiving over the islands, and white-water rafting on the Navua River are just a few of the options available. These activities provide an adrenaline rush and the chance to see Fiji's landscapes from a different perspective. The Yasawa Islands are known for their excellent conditions for windsurfing and kitesurfing, attracting enthusiasts from around the world.

Island hopping is another popular activity for families in Fiji. With over 300 islands to explore, each offering its unique charm, island hopping allows families to experience the diversity of Fiji. The Mamanuca and Yasawa Islands are particularly popular for their stunning beaches and clear waters. Day trips and multi-day tours are available, providing opportunities to snorkel, hike, and relax on some of Fiji's most beautiful islands.

Exploring Fiji's natural beauty further can be achieved through eco-tours and nature walks. These tours provide insights into Fiji's diverse ecosystems and the importance of conservation. Families can learn about the island's flora and fauna, visit marine reserves, and participate in conservation projects such as coral planting and beach clean-ups. These activities foster a sense of environmental awareness and responsibility in children.

Dining in Fiji can be a delightful experience for families, with a range of options to suit all tastes. Fijian cuisine is a blend of indigenous flavors and influences from Indian, Chinese, and European cuisines. Local markets such as the Suva Municipal Market or the Nadi Market are great places to sample fresh produce, seafood, and traditional dishes. Street food stalls and local eateries offer a range of delicious options, from fresh coconut water and tropical fruits to curries and seafood specialties. Trying traditional dishes like kokoda (a marinated raw fish dish) and lovo (food cooked in an underground oven) is a must for any family.

Group Activities for Friends and Families

Fiji is an exceptional destination for group travel, offering a wide range of activities and experiences that cater to friends and families alike. The islands' breathtaking natural beauty, vibrant culture, and warm hospitality make it an ideal place for group adventures and bonding experiences. Whether you are looking for outdoor adventures, cultural immersions, or simply relaxing together in paradise, Fiji has something to offer every group.

One of the most enjoyable group activities in Fiji is island hopping. With over 300 islands to explore, island hopping allows groups to experience the diverse landscapes and unique charms of different islands. The Mamanuca and Yasawa Islands are particularly popular for their stunning beaches, clear waters, and vibrant marine life. Day trips and multi-day tours can be arranged, providing opportunities for snorkeling, swimming, and beach picnics. Many tours include stops at several islands, allowing groups to explore secluded beaches, coral reefs, and traditional villages. The shared experience of discovering new places together strengthens bonds and creates lasting memories.

Snorkeling and diving are must-do activities in Fiji, and they are perfect for groups looking to explore the underwater world. Fiji is home to some of the best coral reefs in the world, teeming with colorful fish, sea turtles, and other marine life. Popular snorkeling spots such as the Coral Coast, the Mamanuca Islands, and the Yasawa Islands offer easy access to vibrant reefs. Many resorts and tour operators provide guided snorkeling tours, ensuring that everyone in the group, regardless of their experience level, can enjoy the beauty of the reefs. For more adventurous groups, scuba diving offers an even closer look at Fiji's underwater treasures. Dive shops and resorts offer courses for beginners and advanced divers, allowing groups to explore famous dive sites like the Great White Wall and the Rainbow Reef.

For groups interested in outdoor adventures, hiking through Fiji's lush rainforests is an excellent option. Trails such as those in Colo-I-Suva Forest Park on Viti Levu and Bouma National Heritage Park on Taveuni provide a chance to see towering trees, vibrant birdlife, and picturesque waterfalls. These hikes vary in difficulty, catering to both casual walkers and experienced hikers. Along the way, groups can take refreshing dips in natural pools, enjoy picnic lunches, and appreciate the tranquility of the forest. The shared experience of hiking through beautiful landscapes and overcoming challenges together creates a sense of camaraderie and accomplishment.

Another thrilling activity for groups is river rafting. The Navua River on Viti Levu offers an exciting rafting experience, with rapids that range from gentle to challenging. Guided rafting tours take groups through some of the most scenic parts of the river, navigating through rapids and calm stretches surrounded by lush rainforest. The adventure of paddling together through the rapids and the joy of floating through tranquil sections provide a mix of excitement and relaxation that is perfect for groups.

Kayaking and paddleboarding are other popular water activities that are suitable for groups. Paddling along the coast or through mangrove forests allows groups to explore hidden coves and secluded beaches. Double kayaks and paddleboards make it easy for friends and family members to paddle together, sharing the experience and the views. Many resorts and tour operators offer guided kayaking tours, providing opportunities to learn about the local ecosystems and wildlife.

For groups seeking cultural experiences, visiting a traditional Fijian village can be a highlight of the trip. Many villages welcome visitors with a traditional kava ceremony, a ritual that involves drinking a beverage made from the kava root. This ceremony is an important part of Fijian culture and provides a unique opportunity to connect with the local community. Village tours often include demonstrations of traditional crafts such as mat weaving, tapa cloth making, and basket weaving. Participating in these activities allows groups to learn about Fijian culture and traditions in an interactive and engaging way.

Attending a meke performance is another way to experience Fijian culture. Meke is a traditional dance that tells stories through song and movement. These performances are often accompanied by rhythmic drumming and chanting, creating a captivating and immersive experience. Many resorts and cultural centers offer meke shows, allowing groups to witness this vibrant aspect of Fijian culture firsthand. The shared experience of watching a meke performance and learning about the stories and traditions behind the dances fosters a deeper appreciation of Fijian culture.

For groups interested in history and nature, a visit to the Fiji Museum in Suva is a must. The museum offers a comprehensive overview of the island's past, with exhibits on the Lapita culture, the arrival of Europeans, and the development of modern Fiji. The museum's collection includes ancient artifacts, traditional Fijian tools, and items from the colonial era. A visit to the museum provides valuable insights into the cultural and historical context of Fiji and can be an educational experience for everyone in the group.

Many resorts in Fiji offer group activities and amenities that ensure everyone is entertained and engaged. These include beach volleyball, tennis, and other sports facilities, as well as organized activities such as cooking classes, dance lessons, and traditional craft workshops. Group yoga and fitness classes are also available, providing opportunities for relaxation and wellness. Family-friendly resorts often have kids' clubs and babysitting services, making it easy for parents to enjoy some time to themselves while the children are entertained and cared for.

Fiji's natural beauty provides the perfect backdrop for group dining experiences. Many resorts offer private dining options that allow groups to enjoy a meal in a secluded and intimate setting. Private beach dinners, where a table is set up on the sand with torches and candles, are particularly popular. Groups can enjoy a gourmet meal under the stars, with the sound of the waves providing a soothing backdrop. Some resorts also offer dining experiences in unique locations, such as a treetop platform or a secluded garden, adding an extra touch of magic to the evening.

For groups seeking relaxation and pampering, Fiji's numerous spas and wellness centers provide the perfect escape. Many resorts have on-site spas that offer a range of treatments, from traditional Fijian massages using coconut oil to luxurious facials and body wraps. Group spa packages are available, allowing everyone to enjoy treatments together in a serene and rejuvenating environment. Yoga and meditation classes are also available at many resorts, often held in scenic outdoor settings that enhance the sense of peace and tranquility.

Exploring Fiji's arts and crafts scene can be a fun and rewarding group activity. Visiting local markets and craft shops allows groups to see and purchase handmade items such as masi (tapa cloth), woven baskets, and wooden carvings. These items make unique and meaningful souvenirs that can remind everyone of their trip to Fiji. Engaging with local artisans and learning about their craft can also be a rewarding experience.

For those looking to explore Fiji's natural beauty further, eco-tours and nature walks are excellent options. These tours provide insights into Fiji's diverse ecosystems and the importance of conservation. Groups can learn about the island's flora and fauna, visit marine reserves, and participate in conservation projects such as coral planting and beach clean-ups. These activities foster a sense of environmental awareness and responsibility and provide opportunities for group bonding.

CHAPTER 6

ACCOMMODATION OPTIONS

Luxury Resorts and Villas

Fiji is renowned for its luxury resorts and villas, offering a range of high-end accommodation options that cater to travelers seeking an exquisite and memorable stay. These resorts and villas are often located in some of the most picturesque settings in the world, surrounded by pristine beaches, lush tropical landscapes, and crystal-clear waters.

One of the defining characteristics of luxury resorts and villas in Fiji is their stunning locations. Many of these properties are situated on private islands or secluded beaches, offering unparalleled privacy and exclusivity. The natural beauty of Fiji serves as a backdrop for these luxurious accommodations, creating a serene and idyllic environment that is perfect for relaxation and rejuvenation. Whether you are staying in a beachfront villa with direct access to the ocean or a hillside resort with panoramic views, the setting of these properties is designed to immerse you in the natural splendor of Fiji.

Luxury resorts and villas in Fiji are renowned for their world-class amenities and services. These properties are designed to provide the utmost comfort and convenience, with spacious and elegantly appointed rooms, private pools, and expansive outdoor living areas. The interiors are often decorated with a blend of contemporary design and traditional Fijian elements, creating a sophisticated yet culturally rich ambiance. High-quality furnishings, premium bedding, and state-of-the-art technology ensure that every aspect of your stay is catered to.

One of the standout features of luxury resorts and villas in Fiji is the personalized service they offer. Many properties provide dedicated butler services, where a personal butler is assigned to attend to your every need. From unpacking your luggage and arranging excursions to serving meals and organizing special events, the butler service ensures that your stay is seamless and stress-free. Additionally, many resorts offer private chefs who can prepare customized meals based on your preferences and dietary requirements. This level of personalized service adds an extra layer of luxury and convenience to your stay.

Dining at luxury resorts and villas in Fiji is an exceptional experience, with a focus on fresh, locally sourced ingredients and innovative culinary techniques. Many properties feature multiple dining venues, ranging from fine dining restaurants to casual beachfront cafes. The menus often highlight Fijian cuisine, incorporating local flavors and traditional dishes. Guests can enjoy gourmet meals in a variety of settings, whether it's a romantic dinner on the beach, a private picnic on a secluded island, or a family meal in the comfort of your villa. Some resorts also offer interactive dining experiences, such as cooking classes and chef's tables, allowing guests to learn about Fijian cuisine and participate in the culinary process.

Wellness and relaxation are key components of the luxury experience in Fiji. Many resorts feature world-class spas that offer a range of treatments and therapies designed to rejuvenate the body and mind. These spas often incorporate traditional Fijian healing practices and natural ingredients, such as coconut oil and tropical herbs, into their treatments. Guests can indulge in massages, facials, body scrubs, and other therapies in serene settings, such as overwater pavilions or beachfront cabanas. In addition to spa services, many resorts offer yoga and meditation classes, fitness centers, and wellness programs that promote holistic well-being.

For those seeking adventure and exploration, luxury resorts and villas in Fiji offer a wide array of activities and excursions. The crystal-clear waters surrounding the islands are perfect for snorkeling, diving, and other water sports. Many resorts have their own dive centers and offer guided diving and snorkeling trips to some of Fiji's most renowned reefs. Kayaking, paddleboarding, and sailing are also popular activities, allowing guests to explore the coastline and nearby islands. For those interested in fishing, deep-sea and sport fishing charters are available.

On land, guests can enjoy hiking and nature walks through the lush rainforests and scenic landscapes of Fiji. Many resorts offer guided tours that provide insights into the local flora and fauna, as well as the cultural and historical significance of the area. Visiting traditional Fijian villages and participating in cultural activities, such as kava ceremonies and meke performances, offer a deeper understanding of Fijian culture and heritage. These experiences are often arranged by the resort, ensuring a seamless and enriching experience for guests.

Privacy and exclusivity are hallmarks of luxury villas in Fiji. These private residences offer a secluded retreat where guests can enjoy their own space without interruption. Villas are typically equipped with all the amenities of a luxury home, including fully equipped kitchens, private pools, and spacious living and dining areas. Many villas also feature outdoor showers, plunge pools, and expansive terraces with breathtaking views. The secluded nature of these villas makes them ideal for romantic getaways, family vacations, and special celebrations.

Luxury resorts and villas in Fiji are also renowned for their commitment to sustainability and environmental conservation. Many properties implement eco-friendly practices, such as using renewable energy sources, reducing waste, and supporting local communities. Resorts often engage in conservation efforts to protect the surrounding marine and terrestrial ecosystems, such as coral reef restoration and wildlife preservation programs. Guests are encouraged to participate in these initiatives, whether through educational programs, volunteer activities, or simply by making environmentally conscious choices during their stay.

Mid-Range Hotels and Lodges

Fiji offers a wide range of accommodation options to suit various budgets and preferences, and mid-range hotels and lodges are particularly popular among travelers seeking comfort, convenience, and value for money. These accommodations provide a balance of quality amenities, friendly service, and an authentic Fijian experience without the high price tag of luxury resorts.

Mid-range hotels and lodges in Fiji are often strategically located in areas that offer both convenience and scenic beauty. Many of these properties are situated near popular beaches, cultural sites, and natural attractions, making them an ideal base for exploring the islands. Whether you choose to stay in the bustling town of Nadi, the capital city of Suva, or on one of the smaller islands, mid-range accommodations provide easy access to the best that Fiji has to offer.

One of the key advantages of mid-range hotels and lodges is their affordability. These accommodations typically offer a range of room types and rates, allowing travelers to choose options that best suit their budget. Despite being more affordable than luxury resorts, mid-range properties still provide a high level of comfort and quality. Rooms are generally well-appointed, featuring comfortable beds, clean linens, and modern amenities such as air conditioning, Wi-

Fi, and flat-screen TVs. Many properties also offer rooms with ocean views, balconies, or direct beach access, enhancing the overall experience.

The facilities at mid-range hotels and lodges are designed to cater to the needs of travelers while providing a relaxed and enjoyable environment. Most properties feature on-site restaurants or cafes that serve a variety of cuisines, including local Fijian dishes and international favorites. Breakfast is often included in the room rate, offering a convenient and cost-effective start to the day. Many hotels also have bars or lounges where guests can unwind with a drink and socialize with fellow travelers.

Swimming pools are a common feature at mid-range accommodations, providing a refreshing alternative to the beach. These pools are typically surrounded by sun loungers and shaded areas, creating a perfect spot for relaxation. Some properties also offer additional recreational facilities such as tennis courts, fitness centers, and game rooms, ensuring that guests have plenty of options for entertainment and exercise during their stay.

For those who enjoy outdoor activities, many mid-range hotels and lodges in Fiji offer easy access to a variety of water sports and excursions. Snorkeling, kayaking, paddleboarding, and fishing are popular activities that can often be arranged directly through the hotel. Many properties also provide equipment rental and guided tours, making it convenient for guests to explore the surrounding waters and marine life. Some hotels even have their own dive centers, offering courses and guided dives for those interested in exploring Fiji's renowned coral reefs.

Mid-range accommodations in Fiji often emphasize personalized service and a warm, welcoming atmosphere. The staff at these properties are typically friendly and attentive, ensuring that guests feel at home during their stay. Many hotels and lodges are family-owned and operated, adding a personal touch to the service. The staff are usually knowledgeable about the local area and can provide valuable recommendations for sightseeing, dining, and activities. This personalized service enhances the overall experience and helps guests make the most of their time in Fiji.

Cultural experiences are an integral part of staying at mid-range hotels and lodges in Fiji. Many properties organize traditional Fijian activities and events, such as kava ceremonies, meke dance performances, and village visits. These experiences provide guests with a deeper understanding of Fijian culture and heritage, adding an enriching dimension to their stay. Participating in these activities allows travelers to connect with the local community and gain insights into the traditional way of life in Fiji.

For those traveling with families, mid-range hotels and lodges offer a range of amenities and services that cater to the needs of both adults and children. Family rooms or suites are often available, providing extra space and convenience for families traveling together. Many properties also offer kids' clubs or activity programs, ensuring that younger guests are entertained and engaged during their stay. Babysitting services are typically available, allowing parents to enjoy some time to themselves while knowing that their children are in good hands.

The dining options at mid-range hotels and lodges in Fiji are diverse and often include a focus on fresh, locally sourced ingredients. On-site restaurants typically offer a mix of Fijian cuisine and international dishes, catering to a variety of tastes and dietary preferences. Guests can enjoy delicious meals in a relaxed and casual setting, with many restaurants offering outdoor seating with beautiful views of the ocean or gardens. The emphasis on local ingredients means that guests have the opportunity to sample traditional Fijian dishes made with fresh seafood, tropical fruits, and locally grown vegetables.

In addition to on-site dining, many mid-range accommodations are located near local restaurants and eateries, allowing guests to explore the local food scene. Markets and street food vendors are also common, offering a range of affordable and tasty options. Trying the local cuisine is an essential part of the Fiji experience, and mid-range accommodations provide the perfect base for culinary exploration.

For travelers interested in eco-friendly and sustainable tourism, many mid-range hotels and lodges in Fiji are committed to environmental conservation and sustainable practices. These properties often implement initiatives such as recycling programs, energy-efficient systems, and water conservation measures. Some hotels also engage in community projects and support local conservation efforts, allowing guests to contribute to the preservation of Fiji's natural beauty and cultural heritage. Staying at an eco-friendly property not only provides a comfortable and enjoyable experience but also aligns with responsible travel principles.

Budget-Friendly Hostels and Guesthouses

Fiji is not only a destination for luxury travelers but also an excellent option for budget-conscious visitors. Budget-friendly hostels and guesthouses offer a great way to experience the beauty and culture of Fiji without spending a fortune. These accommodations provide a range of amenities and services that cater to travelers looking for comfort and affordability.

One of the primary advantages of staying in budget-friendly hostels and guesthouses in Fiji is the significant cost savings. These accommodations offer some of the most affordable lodging options in the country, making them an ideal choice for backpackers, solo travelers, and families on a budget. Despite the lower cost, many hostels and guesthouses provide a high level of comfort and convenience. Rooms are typically clean and well-maintained, featuring comfortable beds, fresh linens, and basic amenities such as Wi-Fi, fans, or air conditioning. Some properties even offer private rooms with en-suite bathrooms, allowing guests to enjoy additional privacy and comfort while still staying within their budget.

Budget-friendly hostels and guesthouses in Fiji often emphasize a friendly and welcoming atmosphere, creating a sense of community among travelers. Common areas such as lounges, kitchens, and outdoor spaces are designed to encourage social interaction, making it easy for guests to meet and connect with fellow travelers. These shared spaces are often equipped with comfortable seating, games, and entertainment options, providing a relaxed environment where guests can unwind and share their travel experiences. This communal aspect of hostels and guesthouses fosters a sense of camaraderie and can lead to lasting friendships.

Many budget accommodations in Fiji are located in convenient and scenic areas, offering easy access to beaches, markets, and local attractions. Staying in a hostel or guesthouse allows travelers to experience the local culture and lifestyle more intimately than they might at a larger, more isolated resort. Guests can explore nearby villages, visit local markets, and dine at family-run restaurants, gaining a deeper appreciation for Fijian culture and hospitality. The central locations of many budget accommodations also make it easy to access public transportation and arrange day trips to nearby islands and attractions.

For those who enjoy outdoor activities, budget-friendly hostels and guesthouses in Fiji often provide easy access to a variety of recreational opportunities. Many properties are located near popular beaches and water sports centers, allowing guests to participate in activities such as snorkeling, kayaking, and paddleboarding. Some hostels and guesthouses offer equipment rental and guided tours, making it convenient for guests to explore the surrounding waters and marine life. Budget travelers can enjoy the same beautiful beaches and clear waters as those staying in luxury resorts, without the high price tag.

Hiking and nature walks are also popular activities for budget travelers in Fiji. Many hostels and guesthouses are situated near scenic trails and natural attractions, providing opportunities for guests to explore the island's lush rainforests, waterfalls, and viewpoints. Hiking through Fiji's diverse landscapes allows travelers to experience the island's natural beauty up close and can be a rewarding and budget-friendly way to spend a day. Some properties offer guided hikes or can provide maps and recommendations for nearby trails, ensuring that guests can make the most of their outdoor adventures.

Cultural experiences are an integral part of staying at budget-friendly hostels and guesthouses in Fiji. Many properties organize traditional Fijian activities and events, such as kava ceremonies, meke dance performances, and cooking classes. These experiences provide guests with a deeper understanding of Fijian culture and heritage, adding an enriching dimension to their stay. Participating in these activities allows travelers to connect with the local community and gain insights into the traditional way of life in Fiji. Additionally, hostel and guesthouse staff are often locals who can share valuable tips and recommendations for exploring the area.

Dining options at budget-friendly hostels and guesthouses are diverse and often include communal kitchens where guests can prepare their own meals. This can be a significant cost-saving measure, as it allows travelers to buy fresh produce and ingredients from local markets and cook their own meals. Communal kitchens are usually well-equipped with basic appliances and utensils, making it easy for guests to prepare a variety of dishes. Sharing meals with fellow travelers in the communal dining area can also be a fun and social experience, providing opportunities to exchange recipes and cooking tips.

Many budget accommodations in Fiji also have on-site cafes or restaurants that serve affordable and delicious meals. These dining options often feature a mix of Fijian cuisine and international dishes, catering to a variety of tastes and dietary preferences. Guests can enjoy hearty breakfasts, light lunches, and satisfying dinners without having to leave the property. Some hostels and guesthouses also offer meal packages that include breakfast or dinner, providing added convenience and value for money.

For travelers interested in eco-friendly and sustainable tourism, many budget-friendly hostels and guesthouses in Fiji are committed to environmental conservation and sustainable practices. These properties often implement initiatives such as recycling programs, energy-efficient systems, and water conservation measures. Some accommodations also engage in community projects and support local conservation efforts, allowing guests to contribute to the preservation of Fiji's natural beauty and cultural heritage. Staying at an eco-friendly property not only provides a comfortable and enjoyable experience but also aligns with responsible travel principles.

Unique Stays: Bures and Eco-Lodges

Fiji offers a diverse range of accommodation options that cater to different preferences and budgets. Among these, unique stays such as bures and eco-lodges stand out for their distinctive charm and commitment to sustainability. These types of accommodations provide guests with an authentic Fijian experience, blending traditional design with modern comforts while emphasizing environmental conservation and cultural appreciation.

Bures are traditional Fijian dwellings that have been adapted to serve as comfortable and unique accommodation options for travelers. Typically constructed from natural materials such as wood, bamboo, and thatch, bures reflect the architectural heritage of Fiji and blend seamlessly with the natural environment. Staying in a bure offers guests an opportunity to experience a slice of traditional Fijian life while enjoying modern amenities and comforts. These structures are often set in picturesque locations, such as beachfronts, gardens, or amidst lush tropical forests, providing a serene and immersive experience.

The design of a bure is characterized by its simplicity and functionality. The use of natural materials ensures that the structures are well-ventilated and blend harmoniously with their surroundings. Inside, bures are typically furnished with comfortable beds, seating areas, and storage space, often adorned with locally crafted decor that adds to the authentic ambiance. While bures may vary in size and luxury, they all provide a cozy and intimate atmosphere that is perfect for relaxation.

Many bures come equipped with modern amenities to ensure a comfortable stay. These may include en-suite bathrooms with hot water, air conditioning or ceiling fans, and private verandas with stunning views. Some bures also feature outdoor showers, allowing guests to enjoy a unique bathing experience under the open sky. The combination of traditional design and modern conveniences makes bures an attractive option for travelers seeking a distinctive and comfortable stay in Fiji.

Eco-lodges, on the other hand, are accommodations that prioritize environmental sustainability and responsible tourism. These lodges are designed to have minimal impact on the environment while providing guests with a high-quality and immersive experience. Eco-lodges in Fiji are often located in areas of natural beauty, such as rainforests, mountains, or coastal regions, offering guests a chance to connect with nature and enjoy a range of outdoor activities.

The construction of eco-lodges typically involves the use of sustainable materials and building practices. Many eco-lodges utilize renewable energy sources such as solar or wind power, implement water conservation measures, and incorporate waste reduction and recycling programs. The aim is to create a sustainable and eco-friendly environment that supports the local ecosystem and reduces the carbon footprint of the accommodation.

Staying at an eco-lodge provides guests with a unique opportunity to learn about and participate in conservation efforts. Many eco-lodges offer educational programs and activities that focus on environmental awareness and sustainability. Guests can engage in activities such as guided nature walks, wildlife watching, and conservation projects like tree planting or coral reef restoration. These experiences not only enhance the overall stay but also contribute to the preservation of Fiji's natural beauty and biodiversity.

In addition to their environmental focus, eco-lodges in Fiji often emphasize cultural appreciation and community engagement. Many lodges work closely with local communities, providing employment opportunities and supporting local businesses. Guests can participate in cultural activities such as traditional Fijian ceremonies, handicraft workshops, and village visits, gaining a deeper understanding of Fijian culture and traditions. This cultural immersion adds a meaningful dimension to the stay, allowing guests to connect with the local way of life.

Both bures and eco-lodges offer a range of amenities and services that cater to the needs of travelers. Many properties feature on-site dining options that highlight fresh, locally sourced ingredients and traditional Fijian cuisine. Guests can enjoy delicious meals in scenic settings, such as beachfront restaurants, garden terraces, or outdoor dining areas with views of the surrounding landscape. The emphasis on local ingredients ensures that the food is fresh and flavorful, providing a taste of Fiji's rich culinary heritage.

For those seeking relaxation and wellness, many bures and eco-lodges offer spa services and wellness programs. These may include traditional Fijian massages, yoga and meditation classes, and other holistic treatments that promote physical and mental well-being. The serene and natural environment of these accommodations provides the perfect backdrop for relaxation and rejuvenation.

Adventure and outdoor activities are also a significant part of the experience at bures and eco-lodges. Guests can engage in a variety of activities such as snorkeling, diving, kayaking, hiking, and birdwatching. The diverse landscapes of Fiji provide ample opportunities for exploration and adventure, whether it's discovering the vibrant coral reefs, trekking through lush rainforests, or paddling along tranquil rivers. The staff at bures and eco-lodges are typically knowledgeable about the local area and can provide recommendations and arrange guided tours to enhance the guest experience.

For those looking to celebrate special occasions, many bures and eco-lodges offer personalized services and packages. Whether it's a romantic honeymoon, a family vacation, or a group retreat, these accommodations can tailor the experience to meet the needs and preferences of their guests. Special arrangements such as private dinners, personalized excursions, and exclusive use of facilities can be made to ensure a memorable and unique stay.

Best Places to Stay for Different Types of Travelers

Fiji offers a wide variety of accommodation options that cater to different types of travelers, each with unique needs and preferences. From luxury resorts and private villas to mid-range hotels, budget-friendly hostels, and eco-lodges, Fiji has something to suit every traveler's taste and budget.

Luxury Travelers

For those seeking an opulent and indulgent experience, Fiji's luxury resorts and private villas offer unparalleled comfort, service, and amenities. These accommodations are often situated in stunning locations, such as private islands or exclusive beachfronts, providing a serene and intimate environment. Properties like the Laucala Island Resort, Likuliku Lagoon Resort, and Vomo Island Resort are renowned for their lavish amenities, including private plunge pools, overwater bungalows, and world-class dining. These resorts offer personalized services such as private butlers, gourmet chefs, and bespoke excursions, ensuring a truly luxurious and unforgettable stay.

Couples and Honeymooners

Fiji is a dream destination for couples and honeymooners, offering a romantic and idyllic setting for a memorable getaway. Many resorts and boutique hotels cater specifically to couples, providing intimate accommodations and exclusive services. The Tokoriki Island Resort, for example, is an adults-only retreat known for its romantic ambiance, private beachfront villas, and candlelit dinners on the beach. The Royal Davui Island Resort is another excellent choice, offering secluded villas, spa treatments, and activities like snorkeling and kayaking, perfect for couples seeking both relaxation and adventure.

Families

Traveling with family requires accommodations that cater to the needs of both adults and children, offering a mix of comfort, convenience, and entertainment. Resorts like the Shangri-La's Fijian Resort & Spa and the Outrigger Fiji Beach Resort are family-friendly properties that provide spacious rooms, kids' clubs, and a variety of activities for all ages. These resorts often feature multiple dining options, swimming pools, and organized excursions, ensuring that every family member has an enjoyable and stress-free vacation. Additionally, many family-friendly resorts offer babysitting services, allowing parents to enjoy some time to themselves.

Adventure Seekers

For adventure enthusiasts, Fiji offers accommodations that provide easy access to a wide range of outdoor activities and excursions. The Yasawa Island Resort and Spa, for instance, is located in an area known for its excellent diving, snorkeling, and hiking opportunities. Similarly, the Jean-Michel Cousteau Resort in Savusavu is renowned for its eco-friendly approach and offers activities like scuba diving, kayaking, and rainforest hikes. These resorts often have in-house dive centers and experienced guides, ensuring that adventure seekers can explore the best of Fiji's natural beauty.

Solo Travelers

Solo travelers looking for a blend of social interaction and personal space will find that hostels and budget-friendly guesthouses are ideal options. Properties like Bamboo Backpackers and Smugglers Cove Beach Resort in Nadi offer affordable accommodation with a vibrant, communal atmosphere. These hostels provide dormitory-style rooms, private rooms, and communal areas where solo travelers can meet others and share travel experiences. Many hostels also organize group activities and tours, making it easy for solo travelers to explore Fiji while making new friends.

Eco-Conscious Travelers

For those who prioritize sustainability and environmental conservation, Fiji's eco-lodges provide a unique and responsible travel experience. Accommodations like the Matava Resort on Kadavu Island and the Taveuni Island Resort & Spa emphasize eco-friendly practices, such as using renewable energy, supporting local communities, and promoting conservation efforts. These eco-lodges offer a range of activities that allow guests to engage with the natural environment, including guided nature walks, wildlife watching, and participation in conservation projects.

Budget Travelers
Budget-conscious travelers will find plenty of affordable accommodation options in Fiji, from guesthouses to budget hotels and hostels. These properties offer clean and comfortable rooms at a fraction of the cost of luxury resorts. Options like the Nadi Bay Resort Hotel and the Beachouse on the Coral Coast provide basic amenities and convenient locations near popular attractions and public transport. Budget accommodations often feature communal kitchens, allowing guests to save money by preparing their own meals, and they frequently organize social events and tours that offer an affordable way to explore the area.

Cultural Enthusiasts

Travelers interested in experiencing the local culture and traditions will appreciate accommodations that provide cultural immersion and interaction with local communities. Staying in traditional Fijian bures or in villages that offer homestays can provide an authentic cultural experience. Accommodations like the Navala Village on Viti Levu offer visitors the chance to live in a traditional thatched-roof house, participate in daily village life, and enjoy traditional Fijian meals. These stays allow travelers to gain a deeper understanding of Fijian culture and hospitality.

Wellness Seekers

For those looking to focus on wellness and relaxation, Fiji's wellness resorts and retreats offer a range of activities and services designed to rejuvenate the mind and body. Properties like the Namale Resort & Spa and the Daku Resort in Savusavu offer wellness programs that include yoga, meditation, spa treatments, and healthy cuisine. These resorts are often set in tranquil environments, such as beachfronts or tropical gardens, providing the perfect backdrop for relaxation and rejuvenation.

CHAPTER 7

EXPERIENCING FIJI'S RICH CULTURE

Traditional Fijian Ceremonies

Traditional Fijian ceremonies are an integral part of Fiji's rich cultural heritage, reflecting the deep-rooted customs and social structures that have shaped Fijian society for centuries. These ceremonies are more than just rituals; they are expressions of community values, respect, and identity.

The most well-known and widely practiced Fijian ceremony is the yaqona, or kava, ceremony. This ritual revolves around the preparation and drinking of kava, a beverage made from the ground root of the kava plant. Kava holds a central place in Fijian culture, symbolizing unity, respect, and social cohesion. The ceremony typically begins with the preparation of the kava root, which is pounded into a fine powder and mixed with water in a large wooden bowl called a tanoa. The mixture is strained and served in a communal cup made from a coconut shell, called a bilo.

The kava ceremony is led by a master of ceremonies, usually a respected elder or chief, who ensures that the protocol is followed. Participants sit in a circle, with the tanoa placed in the center. The master of ceremonies offers the first cup to the highest-ranking person present, often a chief or honored guest. This act of offering and drinking kava is accompanied by chants and claps, which signify respect and acceptance. Each participant drinks from the same bilo, reinforcing the sense of community and shared experience. The kava ceremony is not only a social occasion but also a spiritual one, as it is believed to connect participants with their ancestors and the spirit world.

Another important traditional Fijian ceremony is the meke, a form of dance and storytelling. The meke is performed on special occasions such as festivals, weddings, and welcoming ceremonies. It combines rhythmic movements, chants, and music to convey stories of Fijian history, mythology, and daily life. The dancers, dressed in traditional costumes made from bark cloth, grass, and shells, move in unison to the beat of drums and the sounds of bamboo pipes. The meke is a powerful expression of Fijian identity and cultural pride, and it plays a crucial role in preserving the oral traditions and history of the Fijian people.

The traditional Fijian wedding ceremony, known as a vakamau, is a vibrant and elaborate affair that reflects the customs and values of Fijian society. The ceremony begins with a formal presentation of gifts, known as itatau, from the groom's family to the bride's family. These gifts often include mats, tapa cloth, and food, symbolizing the groom's respect and commitment to the bride's family. The wedding itself is a communal event, with the entire village participating in the celebrations. The bride and groom wear traditional attire, and the ceremony is conducted by a village elder or chief. The exchange of vows and rings is accompanied by prayers and blessings, and the couple is often showered with flower petals as a symbol of fertility and prosperity.

A significant aspect of traditional Fijian ceremonies is the role of the village and community. In Fijian culture, the concept of communal living and mutual support is paramount. Ceremonies such as the magiti, or communal feast, highlight this communal spirit. The magiti is held on various occasions, including weddings, funerals, and festivals. It involves the preparation and sharing of large quantities of food, including traditional dishes like lovo (food cooked in an underground oven) and kokoda (marinated raw fish). The entire community contributes to the preparation and enjoys the feast together, reinforcing social bonds and collective responsibility.

The bula ceremony is another notable Fijian tradition, often conducted to welcome visitors or mark the arrival of important guests. The word "bula" means "life" or "health" and is commonly used as a greeting in Fiji. The ceremony involves a formal reception with speeches, the presentation of gifts, and the performance of meke dances. The guests are invited to partake in a kava ceremony, symbolizing their acceptance into the community and the establishment of mutual respect. The bula ceremony is a reflection of the Fijian value of hospitality and the importance placed on welcoming strangers as friends.

Funeral ceremonies, or iTaukei, in Fijian culture are profound expressions of respect for the deceased and their family. These ceremonies are elaborate and can last several days, involving the entire village. The preparation of the body, known as vakacerecerei, is a sacred duty performed by close family members. The body is then laid in state, allowing the community to pay their respects. The funeral service includes prayers, hymns, and eulogies, followed by the burial. After the burial, a period of mourning, known as mate ni qele, is observed, during which the family receives support and condolences from the community. The iTaukei ceremonies underscore the deep respect Fijians have for their ancestors and the continuity of life and death within the community.

Initiation ceremonies, such as the vakatoga, mark significant milestones in the lives of young Fijians. These ceremonies celebrate the transition from childhood to adulthood and the responsibilities that come with it. The rituals often include traditional teachings, physical endurance tests, and the symbolic passing of knowledge from elders to the younger generation. The vakatoga is a communal event, attended by family members, village elders, and the wider community, reinforcing the collective responsibility in guiding and supporting the youth.

The installation of a chief, or sau, is another vital ceremony in Fijian culture, reflecting the hierarchical structure and governance of traditional Fijian society. The sau is a complex and highly formalized event that involves various rituals and the participation of different clans within the village. The process begins with the selection of the chief, often from a specific lineage, followed by a series of traditional rites, including the kava ceremony, the presentation of symbols of authority, and the acceptance of the new chief by the community. The installation of a chief is not only a political event but also a reaffirmation of cultural values and social cohesion.

In addition to these major ceremonies, there are numerous other traditional practices and rituals that are an integral part of Fijian life. These include the blessing of new homes, agricultural rituals to ensure bountiful harvests, and rites of passage for various stages of life. Each ceremony and ritual is imbued with symbolic meaning and reflects the deep connection between the Fijian people, their land, and their ancestors.

Understanding and participating in traditional Fijian ceremonies provides a unique and enriching experience for visitors. These ceremonies offer a glimpse into the heart of Fijian culture, showcasing the values of respect, community, and spirituality that underpin Fijian society. Whether observing a kava ceremony, participating in a meke dance, or attending a communal feast, visitors can gain a deeper appreciation for the traditions and customs that have shaped Fiji for generations.

Fijian Cuisine: What to Try and Where

Fijian cuisine is a vibrant and integral part of the country's cultural heritage, offering a rich tapestry of flavors and influences. The food in Fiji is characterized by its use of fresh, local ingredients and traditional cooking methods, reflecting the island's bountiful natural resources and diverse cultural influences.

Fijian cuisine is deeply rooted in the island's history and geography. The traditional diet primarily consists of root crops such as taro, cassava, and sweet potatoes, complemented by an abundance of seafood. Coconut, a staple in Fijian cooking, is used in various forms, from coconut milk and cream to grated coconut and coconut oil. The blend of indigenous Fijian and Indo-Fijian influences creates a unique culinary landscape that is both diverse and flavorful.

One of the most iconic dishes in Fijian cuisine is kokoda, a Fijian version of ceviche. Kokoda is made with raw fish marinated in lime or lemon juice, which "cooks" the fish with its acidity. The fish is then mixed with coconut cream, finely chopped onions, tomatoes, chilies, and fresh herbs. The result is a refreshing and tangy dish that perfectly captures the flavors of the sea and the richness of coconut. Kokoda is often served as an appetizer or a light meal, and it can be found in many local restaurants and resorts across Fiji.

Lovo is another traditional Fijian dish that offers a unique culinary experience. Lovo refers to both the cooking method and the feast prepared using this method. It involves cooking food in an underground oven, similar to a Polynesian imu. To prepare a lovo, a pit is dug in the ground, and stones are heated until they are red-hot. The food, typically including marinated meats, fish, and root vegetables, is wrapped in banana or taro leaves and placed on the hot stones. The pit is then covered with earth, and the food is left to cook slowly for several hours. The result is a smoky, tender, and flavorful meal that is often enjoyed during special occasions and celebrations. Many resorts and cultural centers offer lovo feasts, providing visitors with the opportunity to taste this traditional dish.

Another must-try dish in Fiji is palusami, a savory delight made with taro leaves, coconut cream, and various fillings such as fish, meat, or vegetables. The taro leaves are layered and filled with the ingredients, then wrapped into bundles and baked until the leaves are tender and the filling is flavorful. Palusami is a favorite among locals and can be found at local markets, restaurants, and during communal feasts.

For a taste of Fijian street food, try a dish called vakalolo, which is a type of sweet pudding made from grated cassava, coconut, and brown sugar. The mixture is wrapped in banana leaves and steamed until it is soft and sticky. Vakalolo is a popular snack and dessert, often sold at roadside stalls and markets. Its sweet and coconutty flavor makes it a delightful treat.

Rourou, another traditional dish, showcases the versatility of taro leaves. Rourou is made by simmering young taro leaves in coconut milk until they are tender and creamy. This dish is often served as a side dish with fish or meat and is a staple in Fijian households. The rich, velvety texture of rourou pairs beautifully with grilled or fried seafood, creating a satisfying and comforting meal.

Indo-Fijian cuisine also plays a significant role in the culinary landscape of Fiji, bringing vibrant flavors and spices to the table. One of the most popular Indo-Fijian dishes is curry. Fijian curries are typically milder than their Indian counterparts but are rich in flavor and aroma. Made with a variety of meats, fish, and vegetables, these curries are cooked with a blend of spices, coconut milk, and fresh herbs. Roti, a type of flatbread, is commonly served alongside curry, perfect for scooping up the flavorful sauce. You can find delicious curries in many restaurants and local eateries, especially in areas with a significant Indo-Fijian population, such as Suva and Nadi.

For those interested in sampling a variety of Fijian and Indo-Fijian dishes, local markets and food festivals are excellent places to explore. The Suva Municipal Market, the largest market in Fiji, offers a wide array of fresh produce, seafood, and prepared foods. Here, you can sample traditional dishes like kokoda, palusami, and vakalolo, as well as fresh tropical fruits such as pineapple, mango, and papaya. The market is a bustling hub of activity and provides a glimpse into daily life in Fiji.

In addition to traditional dishes, Fiji's culinary scene also includes a range of contemporary and fusion cuisine. Many resorts and high-end restaurants offer modern interpretations of Fijian and Indo-Fijian dishes, incorporating international flavors and techniques. For example, you might find a gourmet version of kokoda served with avocado and microgreens, or a lovo feast featuring a variety of meats and vegetables cooked with innovative marinades and spices. These modern takes on traditional dishes provide a fresh and exciting dining experience while honoring the culinary heritage of Fiji.

For a unique dining experience, consider visiting one of Fiji's eco-resorts or farm-to-table restaurants. These establishments focus on sustainability and locally sourced ingredients, offering fresh and flavorful dishes that showcase the best of Fijian produce. Places like Daku Resort in Savusavu and the Fiji Orchid in Lautoka emphasize the use of organic and seasonal ingredients, creating menus that reflect the natural bounty of the islands. Dining at these eco-conscious venues allows you to enjoy delicious food while supporting sustainable practices and local farmers.

Fijian cuisine is not just about the food itself but also the communal and cultural experience of sharing a meal. Fijians place great importance on hospitality and the act of eating together, which is reflected in their traditional feasts and ceremonies. When visiting Fiji, take the time to participate in a communal meal or feast, whether it's a lovo, a village celebration, or a family gathering. These experiences offer a deeper connection to the culture and provide an opportunity to enjoy authentic Fijian dishes in a warm and welcoming environment.

Visiting Local Villages

Visiting local villages in Fiji offers a unique and enriching experience that allows travelers to immerse themselves in the authentic culture and daily life of the Fijian people. This kind of experience goes beyond the typical tourist attractions, providing deeper insights into the traditions, customs, and community spirit that define Fijian society.

Fijian villages are characterized by their communal living arrangements, where strong social bonds and mutual support are fundamental aspects of daily life. The structure of a typical village often includes a central meeting house, known as the "bure," which serves as a focal point for community gatherings, ceremonies, and important discussions. Surrounding the bure are family homes, built in traditional or modern styles, often made from local materials such as wood, bamboo, and thatch. The layout of the village is designed to promote a sense of community and togetherness, with open spaces for communal activities and gardens for growing food.

When visiting a Fijian village, it is important to understand and respect the local customs and etiquette. Visitors are typically welcomed with a formal greeting, often involving a kava ceremony, which is a central part of Fijian hospitality. The kava ceremony is a traditional ritual where kava, a beverage made from the ground root of the kava plant, is prepared and shared among participants. This ceremony symbolizes respect, unity, and social bonding. During the ceremony, the kava is mixed with water in a large wooden bowl and served in a communal cup called a bilo. Participants sit in a circle, with the highest-ranking person or chief receiving the first cup. The ceremony is accompanied by chants and claps, creating a solemn and respectful atmosphere.

As a visitor, it is essential to dress modestly and appropriately when visiting a village. Women should wear skirts or dresses that cover the knees and avoid sleeveless tops, while men should wear sulu (a traditional Fijian wraparound skirt) or long trousers and a shirt. This dress code demonstrates respect for the local culture and customs. Additionally, it is customary to remove your shoes before entering a home or the bure.

One of the highlights of visiting a Fijian village is the opportunity to interact with the local people and participate in their daily activities. Fijians are known for their warm hospitality and friendliness, and visitors are often invited to join in various aspects of village life. This can include helping with cooking traditional meals, learning how to weave mats or baskets, or participating in communal farming activities. These hands-on experiences provide a deeper understanding of Fijian traditions and the importance of community cooperation.

Fijian cuisine plays a central role in village life, and sharing a meal with the villagers is a common and cherished experience. Traditional Fijian meals often include dishes such as lovo (food cooked in an underground oven), rourou (taro leaves cooked in coconut milk), and fresh seafood. Meals are typically served on a mat on the floor, and everyone eats together, reinforcing the sense of community. Visitors are encouraged to try the local dishes and learn about the ingredients and cooking methods used.

In addition to everyday activities, many villages hold cultural performances and ceremonies that visitors can observe or participate in. These include traditional dances known as meke, where villagers perform rhythmic movements and chants to the accompaniment of drums and bamboo pipes. Meke dances tell stories of Fijian history, mythology, and daily life, and are performed with great energy and enthusiasm. Participating in or watching a meke performance offers a captivating insight into Fijian cultural expression and storytelling.

Education and religion also play significant roles in Fijian village life. Most villages have a school where children receive their primary education, often taught in both English and Fijian. Visitors may have the opportunity to visit the school, meet the teachers and students, and learn about the education system in Fiji. Additionally, many villages have a church, reflecting the strong Christian faith that is prevalent in Fijian society. Attending a Sunday service or other religious events can provide insights into the spiritual life of the community and the importance of faith in daily life.

Handicrafts and traditional arts are another important aspect of Fijian village culture. Villagers are skilled in various crafts such as mat weaving, tapa cloth making, and wood carving. These crafts are not only functional but also hold cultural and symbolic significance. Visitors can watch artisans at work, learn about the techniques and materials used, and even try their hand at creating their own pieces. Purchasing locally made handicrafts directly from the artisans supports the local economy and preserves these traditional skills.

Visiting a Fijian village also offers an opportunity to learn about the traditional governance system and the role of the chief. The chief, or "turaga," is a respected leader who plays a crucial role in maintaining order, resolving disputes, and representing the village in broader community matters. The installation of a chief is a significant event, marked by various ceremonies and rituals that emphasize the importance of leadership and continuity. Understanding the chief's role and the governance structure provides deeper insights into the social organization of Fijian villages.

For those interested in environmental conservation, many Fijian villages are actively involved in preserving their natural surroundings and promoting sustainable practices. Visitors can learn about these efforts, which may include marine conservation projects, reforestation initiatives, and sustainable farming practices. Participating in conservation activities, such as planting trees or helping with beach clean-ups, allows visitors to contribute positively to the community and the environment.

The Art of Fijian Handicrafts

The art of Fijian handicrafts is a rich and intricate part of Fiji's cultural heritage, embodying centuries of tradition, skill, and creativity. Handicrafts in Fiji are not just items of utility or decoration; they are expressions of cultural identity, community values, and artistic excellence.

Fijian handicrafts are known for their beauty, craftsmanship, and the use of natural materials. Among the most iconic of these crafts is the masi, also known as tapa cloth. Masi is made from the bark of the mulberry tree, which is soaked, beaten, and then felted together to create a durable fabric. The process of making masi is labor-intensive and requires a high level of skill. Once the cloth is prepared, it is decorated with traditional patterns and designs using natural dyes. These designs often have symbolic meanings and can represent various aspects of Fijian life, such as social status, family heritage, and spiritual beliefs. Masi is used for a variety of purposes, including clothing, ceremonial items, and wall hangings, and is highly prized for its cultural significance and artistic beauty.

Another prominent Fijian handicraft is mat weaving. Mats, or "kuta," are woven from the leaves of the pandanus or pandan plant. The leaves are harvested, boiled, and dried before being stripped into thin fibers. These fibers are then intricately woven by hand into mats of various sizes and patterns. Mat weaving is traditionally done by women and is an important communal activity in Fijian villages. The mats are used in everyday life for sleeping, sitting, and as gifts during important ceremonies and events. The skill of mat weaving is passed down through generations, and the mats themselves are often treasured family heirlooms.

Fijian wood carving is another traditional craft that showcases the artistry and skill of Fijian artisans. Carved items include bowls, war clubs, kava bowls, and figurines, often made from native hardwoods such as vesi and dakua. The designs on these items are typically geometric and stylized, reflecting traditional Fijian aesthetics. Wood carving is predominantly done by men and requires a deep understanding of the material and the tools used. The process involves carefully selecting the wood, carving it into the desired shape, and then finishing it with sandpaper and natural oils. Each piece is unique and often imbued with cultural significance, making Fijian wood carvings highly valued both locally and internationally.

Basket weaving is another traditional craft in Fiji, using materials such as coconut leaves, pandanus leaves, and reeds. Baskets are woven in various shapes and sizes and are used for practical purposes such as carrying goods, storing food, and fishing. The weaving patterns are complex and require significant skill and patience. Basket weaving is often done in communal settings, with multiple generations working together and sharing techniques and stories. The baskets are not only functional but also serve as a symbol of Fijian craftsmanship and resourcefulness.

Fijian pottery is a craft with ancient roots, dating back to the early Lapita culture that first settled the islands. Traditional Fijian pottery is made using clay, which is shaped by hand into pots, bowls, and other vessels. The clay is then fired in open-air kilns, giving the pottery its distinctive texture and color. Pottery is often decorated with incised patterns and natural pigments, creating visually striking and functional pieces. This craft is primarily practiced in the highland regions of Fiji, where the necessary clay deposits are found. Pottery plays a significant role in Fijian culture, particularly in cooking and ceremonial contexts.

One cannot discuss Fijian handicrafts without mentioning the creation of traditional Fijian jewelry. Jewelry is often made from natural materials such as shells, pearls, coconut shell, and whale bone. These materials are carefully crafted into necklaces, bracelets, earrings, and other adornments. Each piece of jewelry often carries cultural symbolism and is worn during special occasions and ceremonies. The process of making jewelry involves intricate carving, polishing, and sometimes the addition of decorative elements like beads and feathers.

The production of traditional Fijian handicrafts is deeply intertwined with the social and cultural fabric of Fijian life. Many of these crafts are produced within the context of communal living, where skills are passed down through generations, and the process of making the items is as important as the final product. Handicrafts are often made during social gatherings, allowing artisans to share knowledge, support each other, and strengthen community bonds. This communal aspect of Fijian handicraft production reinforces the values of cooperation, respect, and cultural continuity.

Visitors to Fiji can explore and purchase these beautiful handicrafts at various locations across the islands. Local markets, such as the Suva Municipal Market and the Nadi Handicraft Market, offer a wide range of traditional items, providing an excellent opportunity to see and buy authentic Fijian crafts. These markets are vibrant and bustling, with vendors displaying their handmade goods and often demonstrating their crafting techniques. Buying directly from the artisans supports the local economy and ensures that the crafts are genuine and ethically sourced.

In addition to markets, many cultural centers and villages welcome visitors to learn about and participate in traditional handicraft-making processes. Places like the Fiji Museum in

Suva and the Arts Village in Pacific Harbour offer workshops and demonstrations, allowing visitors to try their hand at weaving, carving, and other crafts. These interactive experiences provide a deeper appreciation for the skill and effort involved in creating Fijian handicrafts and offer a unique and memorable way to connect with Fijian culture.

Supporting Fijian handicrafts is also about preserving cultural heritage and ensuring that traditional skills are passed on to future generations. Many initiatives and organizations in Fiji are dedicated to promoting and preserving traditional arts and crafts. These efforts include providing training and resources to artisans, creating platforms for selling their products, and raising awareness about the cultural significance of handicrafts. By supporting these initiatives, visitors and collectors can help sustain the rich tradition of Fijian craftsmanship.

Fijian Festivals and Events

Fijian festivals and events are vibrant celebrations that reflect the rich cultural diversity and traditions of Fiji. These gatherings offer a unique opportunity to experience the essence of Fijian life, from its deep-rooted customs and religious practices to its joyous expressions of community spirit and creativity.

One of the most significant and widely celebrated events in Fiji is the Hibiscus Festival. Held annually in Suva, the capital city, the Hibiscus Festival is the largest and oldest festival in Fiji, often referred to as the "Mother of All Festivals." The festival spans over a week and includes a variety of activities and events that attract thousands of locals and tourists. The highlights of the Hibiscus Festival include the beauty pageant, where contestants compete for the title of Miss Hibiscus, cultural performances, food stalls, amusement rides, and live music. The festival showcases the best of Fijian culture and entertainment, providing a platform for local artists, performers, and businesses. The Hibiscus Festival is a celebration of community and cultural pride, drawing people together in a spirit of joy and festivity.

Another major event in Fiji is the Bula Festival, held annually in Nadi. The word "Bula" means "life" or "hello" in Fijian, and the festival is a vibrant celebration of life and the Fijian way of greeting and welcoming people. The Bula Festival features a week-long program of activities, including cultural performances, parades, sports competitions, and beauty pageants. The event also includes food and craft stalls, where visitors can sample traditional Fijian cuisine and purchase handmade crafts. The Bula Festival is a reflection of the warmth and hospitality of the Fijian people, offering visitors a chance to immerse themselves in the local culture and enjoy the lively atmosphere.

Fiji Day is another significant event in the Fijian calendar, celebrated on October 10th each year. Fiji Day marks the anniversary of Fiji's independence from British colonial rule in 1970. The day is observed with national pride and patriotism, featuring ceremonies, parades, and cultural performances across the country. The main celebrations take place in Suva, where government officials and dignitaries participate in the official ceremonies. Fiji Day is a time for Fijians to reflect on their history and achievements and to celebrate their national identity and unity.

The South Pacific's largest Hindu festival, Holi, is also celebrated with great enthusiasm in Fiji, particularly among the Indo-Fijian community. Holi, the festival of colors, is a joyful and exuberant event that signifies the arrival of spring and the triumph of good over evil. During Holi, people gather to throw colored powders and water at each other, sing and dance, and share festive foods. The celebrations often take place in open spaces and community centers, creating a vibrant and colorful spectacle. Holi in Fiji is a testament to the cultural diversity of the country and the harmonious coexistence of different religious and ethnic groups.

Another important Hindu festival celebrated in Fiji is Diwali, the festival of lights. Diwali is a five-day festival that celebrates the victory of light over darkness and good over evil. During Diwali, homes and public places are decorated with oil lamps, candles, and colorful rangoli patterns. Fireworks light up the night sky, and families come together to exchange gifts and enjoy festive meals. The celebrations also include prayers and rituals at temples, as well as cultural performances and community events. Diwali is a time of joy, reflection, and renewal, and it is celebrated with great enthusiasm by the Indo-Fijian community.

Fiji also hosts a variety of traditional Fijian ceremonies and events that offer insights into the island's indigenous culture. One such event is the annual Firewalking Ceremony, held on Beqa Island. The Firewalking Ceremony is a traditional ritual of the Sawau tribe, where men walk barefoot over hot stones without sustaining any injuries. This remarkable feat is performed as a demonstration of faith and spiritual strength, and it is believed to be a way of invoking the protection of ancestral spirits. The ceremony is accompanied by traditional chants, dances, and the drinking of kava. Visitors to Beqa Island can witness this awe-inspiring event and learn about the spiritual and cultural significance of firewalking.

The National Agricultural Show is another notable event in Fiji, showcasing the country's agricultural heritage and promoting sustainable farming practices. The show features exhibits of livestock, crops, and agricultural products, as well as demonstrations of farming techniques and technologies. The event also includes competitions, cultural performances, and educational workshops. The National Agricultural Show provides a platform for farmers, agricultural experts, and the general public to exchange knowledge and ideas, and it highlights the importance of agriculture in Fiji's economy and way of life.

For sports enthusiasts, the Fiji International Golf Tournament is a major event that attracts top golfers from around the world. Held at the Natadola Bay Championship Golf Course, the tournament offers stunning views of the Coral Coast and provides an opportunity for golf fans to see world-class players in action. The event also includes various social and entertainment activities, making it a highlight of Fiji's sporting calendar.

The Fiji International Jazz and Blues Festival is another event that brings a touch of global culture to the islands. Held in Denarau, the festival features performances by local and international jazz and blues artists, offering a diverse and eclectic musical experience. The festival includes concerts, workshops, and jam sessions, creating a lively and vibrant atmosphere for music lovers. The Fiji International Jazz and Blues Festival is a celebration of music and creativity, attracting visitors from all over the world.

The Festival of Pacific Arts, also known as FestPac, is a significant cultural event that brings together artists and performers from across the Pacific region. Hosted by different Pacific countries every four years, FestPac showcases the rich cultural heritage and artistic expressions of the Pacific Islands. The festival includes traditional and contemporary performances, exhibitions, workshops, and cultural exchanges. Fiji has participated in FestPac since its inception and has also had the honor of hosting the event. FestPac is a celebration of Pacific identity and unity, promoting cultural diversity and understanding.

Fiji's New Year celebrations, known as Vaka Viti, are a blend of traditional and modern festivities. The New Year is welcomed with fireworks, parties, and communal feasts. Traditional Fijian rituals, such as the presentation of kava and the performance of meke dances, are also part of the celebrations. Vaka Viti is a time for Fijians to come together with family and friends, reflecting on the past year and looking forward to new beginnings.

In addition to these major festivals and events, Fiji hosts numerous smaller community celebrations, cultural fairs, and religious observances throughout the year. These events provide a glimpse into the daily life and cultural practices of Fijians and offer visitors the chance to engage with the local community.

Basic Fijian Phrases

Traveling to Fiji offers a wonderful opportunity to immerse yourself in a rich cultural experience, and knowing some basic Fijian phrases can greatly enhance your trip. Understanding and using these phrases will not only help you navigate daily interactions but also show respect and appreciation for the local culture.

Fijian, also known as iTaukei, is one of the official languages of Fiji, alongside English and Hindi. While English is widely spoken and understood throughout the islands, using Fijian phrases can create a deeper connection with the local people and enrich your travel experience. Here are some fundamental Fijian phrases to help you get started.

"Bula" (pronounced boo-lah) is perhaps the most well-known Fijian word, and it means "hello" or "welcome." It is used as a greeting in both formal and informal situations and is often accompanied by a warm smile. Saying "Bula" when you meet someone is a simple yet powerful way to express friendliness and goodwill. You will hear this word frequently during your stay in Fiji, and it is likely to become a natural part of your interactions.

"Vinaka" (pronounced vee-nah-kah) means "thank you." This phrase is essential for expressing gratitude and appreciation. Whether you are thanking someone for their help, a meal, or a service, saying "Vinaka" is a polite and respectful way to acknowledge their kindness. You can also use "Vinaka vakalevu" (pronounced vee-nah-kah vah-kah-lay-voo) to say "thank you very much" when you want to convey even greater appreciation.

"Yadra" (pronounced yahndra) means "good morning," while "Moce" (pronounced mo-thay) means "goodbye" or "good night." Using these phrases at the appropriate times of day helps create a friendly and courteous atmosphere. "Yadra" can be used when greeting someone in the morning, and "Moce" is suitable for farewells or when wishing someone a good night's rest.

"Isa" (pronounced ee-sah) is an expression of empathy, sympathy, or fondness. It is often used to convey feelings of sadness, nostalgia, or affection. For example, if someone shares a story about a difficult experience, you might say "Isa" to show that you understand and sympathize with their situation. It can also be used when expressing affection or fond memories.

"Toso" (pronounced toh-soh) means "move" or "go ahead." This phrase is useful in various contexts, such as encouraging someone to proceed or giving directions. For example, if you are guiding someone through a crowded area, you might say "Toso" to indicate that they should move forward. It is a practical phrase to know for everyday interactions.

"Kerekere" (pronounced keh-reh-keh-reh) means "please" or "excuse me." This phrase is essential for making polite requests and showing courtesy. Whether you are asking for assistance, ordering food, or trying to get someone's attention, using "Kerekere" will help you communicate respectfully and effectively. It is a versatile and valuable phrase for maintaining politeness in various situations.

"Sega" (pronounced seh-nga) means "no" or "none," while "Io" (pronounced ee-oh) means "yes." These basic responses are crucial for answering questions and making decisions. Being able to say "Sega" and "Io" will help you navigate conversations and express your preferences clearly. They are simple yet powerful words that facilitate effective communication.

"Au via..." (pronounced ow vee-ah) means "I want..." or "I would like..." This phrase is useful for expressing your needs and desires. For example, if you want to order a specific dish at a restaurant, you might say "Au via kana" (pronounced ow vee-ah kah-nah), which means "I want to eat." Similarly, if you need help with something, you could say "Au via vukei" (pronounced ow vee-ah voo-kei), which means "I want help." Using this phrase helps you articulate your intentions and requests.

"Sa donu" (pronounced sah doh-noo) means "that's correct" or "that's right." This phrase is handy for confirming information or agreeing with someone. It shows that you understand and acknowledge what has been said. For instance, if someone gives you directions and you understand them, you can say "Sa donu" to indicate that the information is correct.

"Vakarau" (pronounced vah-kah-rah-oo) means "prepare" or "get ready." This phrase can be used to indicate that you or someone else should prepare for something. For example, if you are getting ready to leave for an excursion, you might say "Vakarau" to remind everyone to get ready. It is a practical word for organizing activities and ensuring everyone is prepared.

"Rogoca" (pronounced roh-goh-thah) means "listen" or "hear." This phrase is useful for getting someone's attention or asking them to pay attention. For example, if you are giving instructions or telling a story, you might say "Rogoca" to ensure that your audience is listening. It is a straightforward way to engage others in conversation and ensure effective communication.

"Dou bula vinaka" (pronounced doh boo-lah vee-nah-kah) is a more formal greeting that means "hello everyone" or "greetings to all." This phrase is used when addressing a group of people and is a respectful way to acknowledge everyone present. It is especially useful in formal settings or when speaking to a larger audience.

"Vosa vaka-Viti" (pronounced voh-sah vah-kah vee-tee) means "speak Fijian" or "Fijian language." If you want to ask someone to speak in Fijian, you can say "Kerekere, vosa vaka-Viti" (please, speak Fijian). This phrase shows your interest in the language and your willingness to engage with the local culture. It is a way to encourage the use of Fijian in conversation and demonstrate your respect for the language.

These basic Fijian phrases provide a foundation for effective communication and cultural appreciation while traveling in Fiji. By learning and using these phrases, you will be able to navigate everyday interactions with ease and show respect for the local culture. The Fijian people are known for their warmth and hospitality, and speaking even a few words of their language can enhance your travel experience and create meaningful connections.

In addition to these phrases, it is important to understand some cultural norms and etiquette when interacting with Fijians. Respect for elders and community leaders is deeply ingrained in Fijian society. When meeting someone older or of higher status, it is customary to show deference and use formal greetings. Using phrases like "Turaga" (chief) or "Marama" (lady) when addressing someone of high rank demonstrates respect and politeness.

Fijian culture places a strong emphasis on community and communal living. When visiting a village or participating in a communal event, it is important to follow the customs and practices of the community. This includes dressing modestly, removing your shoes before entering a home or the bure, and participating in traditional ceremonies and activities with respect and humility.

The kava ceremony, in particular, is a significant cultural ritual that requires understanding and adherence to proper etiquette. When participating in a kava ceremony, it is important to sit quietly and respectfully, follow the instructions of the master of ceremonies, and accept the kava cup with both hands. Drinking the kava and participating in the ceremony is a way to show respect and acceptance of Fijian hospitality.

CHAPTER 8

BEACHES AND WATER ACTIVITIES

Best Beaches for Relaxation

Fiji is renowned for its breathtaking beaches, where soft white sands meet the crystal-clear waters of the South Pacific. These beaches offer the perfect setting for relaxation, with their serene environments, gentle waves, and stunning natural beauty. Whether you are seeking solitude, picturesque views, or the gentle lapping of waves, Fiji's beaches provide an ideal escape from the hustle and bustle of everyday life. This detailed explanation will explore the best beaches for relaxation in Fiji, providing valuable insights into their unique features and why they are perfect for unwinding and rejuvenating.

One of the most famous beaches in Fiji is Natadola Beach, located on the main island of Viti Levu. Natadola Beach is often described as one of the best beaches in the world, and it's easy to see why. The beach stretches for miles with its pristine white sands and clear turquoise waters. The gentle waves make it perfect for swimming, while the swaying palm trees provide ample shade for those looking to relax on the shore. Natadola Beach is also home to some luxurious resorts, offering spa services, beachfront dining, and other amenities that enhance the relaxation experience. Visitors can take long walks along the beach, bask in the sun, or simply enjoy the soothing sound of the waves.

Yasawa Island is another prime destination for those seeking a tranquil beach experience. The Yasawa Islands are a group of volcanic islands in northwest Fiji, known for their stunning landscapes and secluded beaches. Among them, Blue Lagoon Beach stands out as a true gem. The beach is named after the azure waters of the Blue Lagoon, which are so clear that you can see the vibrant marine life swimming beneath the surface. The soft, powdery sands and the calm, warm waters make it an idyllic spot for swimming, snorkeling, or simply lounging on the beach. The Yasawa Islands are less commercialized than some other parts of Fiji, providing a more intimate and peaceful atmosphere for relaxation.

Another exquisite beach in the Yasawa Islands is Champagne Beach. This beach is known for its pristine sands that resemble fine champagne bubbles when the tide is right. The beach is surrounded by lush vegetation and offers stunning views of the surrounding islands and the open sea. Champagne Beach is a perfect spot for a quiet day of relaxation, with plenty of shade from the trees and the gentle sound of the waves creating a soothing ambiance. The crystal-clear waters are ideal for a refreshing swim, and the beach's remote location ensures a peaceful and uncrowded experience.

On the island of Taveuni, often referred to as the "Garden Island of Fiji," you'll find the beautiful Lavena Beach. This beach is part of the Bouma National Heritage Park, known for its lush rainforests, waterfalls, and stunning coastal views. Lavena Beach is unique in that it combines the beauty of the beach with the allure of the surrounding natural environment. The soft, white sands and clear waters are perfect for relaxation, while the nearby hiking trails and waterfalls offer opportunities for exploration and adventure. Visitors can enjoy a peaceful day on the beach, followed by a refreshing swim in the nearby waterfall pools. Lavena Beach provides a perfect blend of relaxation and natural beauty, making it a must-visit destination in Fiji.

On the Coral Coast of Viti Levu, you'll find the serene Hideaway Beach. This beach is part of the Fiji Hideaway Resort, which offers a range of amenities and activities for guests. Hideaway Beach is known for its tranquil atmosphere, with calm waters and soft sands that invite relaxation. The beach is surrounded by coral reefs, making it an excellent spot for snorkeling and exploring the underwater world. The resort provides beachfront lounges, hammocks, and shaded areas, ensuring that visitors can relax in comfort. Hideaway Beach is perfect for those looking to unwind in a beautiful setting with all the conveniences of a resort.

Matamanoa Island, located in the Mamanuca Islands, offers another perfect beach for relaxation. The island is known for its secluded and pristine beaches, with soft white sands and clear blue waters. The main beach on Matamanoa Island is a haven of tranquility, with its gently swaying palm trees and inviting waters. The island is home to the Matamanoa Island Resort, which provides a range of amenities and activities designed for relaxation. Visitors can enjoy a massage on the beach, take a dip in the infinity pool overlooking the ocean, or simply relax on a sun lounger with a good book. The serene environment and beautiful scenery make Matamanoa Island an ideal destination for a relaxing beach getaway.

On the island of Kadavu, you'll find the picturesque Waisalima Beach. Kadavu is known for its unspoiled beauty and rich marine life, making it a popular destination for divers and nature lovers. Waisalima Beach offers a tranquil and secluded spot for relaxation, with its pristine sands and clear waters. The beach is surrounded by lush vegetation and offers stunning views of the coral reefs just offshore. Visitors can enjoy a peaceful day on the beach, snorkeling in the vibrant coral gardens or simply soaking up the sun. Waisalima Beach is perfect for those looking to escape the crowds and enjoy the natural beauty of Fiji.

Another hidden gem in Fiji is Qamea Island, located near Taveuni. Qamea Island is home to some of the most beautiful and secluded beaches in Fiji, with soft white sands and crystal-clear waters. The beaches on Qamea Island are perfect for relaxation, with their tranquil atmosphere and stunning views. The island is also home to the Qamea Resort and Spa, which offers luxurious beachfront accommodations and a range of wellness and relaxation services. Visitors can enjoy a massage on the beach, take a yoga class overlooking the ocean, or simply relax in a hammock under the palm trees. Qamea Island is a perfect destination for those looking to unwind in a beautiful and peaceful setting.

In the Northern Islands, you'll find the stunning Vomo Island. Vomo Island is known for its pristine beaches, clear waters, and luxurious accommodations. The main beach on Vomo Island is a stretch of soft white sand surrounded by turquoise waters and lush vegetation. The island is home to the Vomo Island Resort, which offers a range of amenities and activities designed for relaxation. Visitors can enjoy a spa treatment on the beach, take a dip in the infinity pool, or simply relax on a sun lounger with a refreshing drink. The serene environment and beautiful scenery make Vomo Island an ideal destination for a relaxing beach getaway.

Top Spots for Snorkeling and Diving

Fiji is renowned worldwide for its stunning underwater landscapes, making it a premier destination for snorkeling and diving enthusiasts. The archipelago boasts some of the most vibrant coral reefs, diverse marine life, and crystal-clear waters that offer unparalleled visibility.

One of the most famous diving destinations in Fiji is the Great Astrolabe Reef, located off the coast of Kadavu Island. This reef is one of the largest barrier reefs in the world, stretching over 100 kilometers. The Great Astrolabe Reef is known for its incredible biodiversity, including an array of hard and soft corals, reef fish, and larger marine creatures such as manta rays, sharks, and turtles. The reef's vibrant coral gardens are a snorkeler's paradise, with shallow areas that are easily accessible and teeming with life. For divers, the reef offers numerous dive sites with varying depths and underwater topographies, including walls, pinnacles, and swim-throughs. The visibility is often excellent, allowing for breathtaking views of the underwater scenery.

Another top spot for diving and snorkeling in Fiji is the Somosomo Strait, located between the islands of Taveuni and Vanua Levu. This strait is home to the famous Rainbow Reef, named for its dazzling array of colorful corals. The Rainbow Reef is renowned for its soft coral displays, often described as the "Soft Coral Capital of the World." The Great White Wall is one of the most iconic dive sites here, featuring a vertical drop covered in white soft corals that glow in the light. Other notable sites include the Purple Wall, known for its vibrant purple corals, and the Fish Factory, which attracts a variety of reef fish. Snorkelers can also enjoy the shallow coral gardens near the shore, where they can encounter an abundance of marine life.

Bligh Water, situated between Viti Levu and Vanua Levu, is another exceptional diving destination in Fiji. Known for its nutrient-rich waters, Bligh Water attracts a diverse range of marine species. The area is famous for its dramatic underwater landscapes, including deep drop-offs, pinnacles, and bommies (coral outcrops). Dive sites such as E6, known for its cathedral-like swim-throughs and vibrant corals, and the Black Magic Mountain, where divers can encounter schools of barracuda and trevally, offer thrilling experiences for advanced divers. The nutrient flow through Bligh Water also brings in larger pelagic species, making it possible to see sharks, manta rays, and even the occasional whale.

Beqa Lagoon, located off the southern coast of Viti Levu, is another must-visit spot for divers and snorkelers. The lagoon is surrounded by a barrier reef that creates calm, protected waters ideal for underwater exploration. Beqa Lagoon is particularly famous for its shark dives, where divers can encounter several species of sharks, including bull sharks, tiger sharks, and reef sharks, in a controlled and safe environment. Besides shark diving, the lagoon offers beautiful coral reefs, wrecks, and vibrant marine life, making it a versatile diving destination. Snorkelers can also enjoy the shallow coral gardens and abundant fish life close to the surface.

The Mamanuca Islands, located west of Nadi, offer some of the best snorkeling and diving experiences in Fiji. The islands are surrounded by clear turquoise waters and pristine coral reefs. Sites such as the Supermarket, a popular spot for shark encounters, and the Pinnacles, known for its stunning coral formations and marine diversity, are highlights for divers. The calm, shallow waters around the islands are perfect for snorkeling, with coral gardens that are home to colorful fish, anemones, and other marine life. The Mamanuca Islands are also easily accessible, making them a convenient option for visitors looking to explore Fiji's underwater beauty.

The Namena Marine Reserve, located off the coast of Vanua Levu, is a protected marine area that offers some of the best diving and snorkeling in Fiji. The reserve is known for its healthy coral reefs, diverse marine life, and excellent visibility. Dive sites such as Chimneys, known for its towering coral structures and abundant marine life, and the Grand Central Station, where divers can encounter large pelagic species, provide thrilling underwater experiences. The Namena Marine Reserve is a haven for biodiversity, with over 1,000 species of fish and numerous species of coral. Snorkelers can also enjoy the shallow reefs near the surface, where they can see a variety of colorful fish and corals.

Vatu-i-Ra Passage, situated between Viti Levu and Vanua Levu, is another top diving destination in Fiji. This passage is known for its strong currents, which bring nutrient-rich waters that support a diverse and vibrant marine ecosystem. The dive sites here, such as Mellow Yellow and Instant Replay, are famous for their stunning soft corals, large schools of fish, and frequent sightings of sharks and manta rays. The strong currents make Vatu-i-Ra Passage more suitable for experienced divers, but the rewards are worth it, with some of the most spectacular underwater scenery in Fiji.

The Lau Islands, located in the eastern part of Fiji, offer remote and pristine diving and snorkeling experiences. The islands are less visited than other parts of Fiji, providing a more untouched and secluded environment. The coral reefs around the Lau Islands are known for their incredible biodiversity, including numerous species of hard and soft corals, reef fish, and larger marine creatures. The crystal-clear waters provide excellent visibility, making it a perfect destination for underwater photography. The remoteness of the Lau Islands adds to the sense of adventure and discovery, making it a unique destination for divers and snorkelers.

For those looking for a unique snorkeling experience, the Great Sea Reef, also known as Cakaulevu, offers an incredible opportunity to explore one of the longest barrier reefs in the world. Located off the northern coast of Vanua Levu, the Great Sea Reef is home to a diverse range of marine life, including numerous species of fish, corals, and invertebrates. The shallow waters and extensive reef system make it ideal for snorkeling, allowing visitors to get up close to the vibrant marine ecosystem. The reef's remoteness and pristine condition make it a hidden gem for underwater exploration.

Sailing and Yachting Adventures

Fiji is a sailor's paradise, offering a vast expanse of turquoise waters, idyllic islands, and steady trade winds that create perfect conditions for sailing and yachting adventures. With over 300 islands scattered across the South Pacific, Fiji provides endless opportunities for exploration, relaxation, and unforgettable maritime experiences. This comprehensive explanation will delve into the allure of sailing and yachting in Fiji, highlighting the key destinations, experiences, and practical information that make it a premier choice for maritime enthusiasts.

One of the primary attractions of sailing and yachting in Fiji is the sheer beauty and diversity of its islands and waters. The Mamanuca and Yasawa Islands, located to the west of the main island of Viti Levu, are among the most popular sailing destinations. These islands are renowned for their stunning beaches, crystal-clear waters, and vibrant coral reefs. Sailing through the Mamanuca Islands offers a chance to visit iconic spots like Cloud 9, a floating bar and pizzeria surrounded by azure waters, and Monuriki Island, made famous by the movie "Cast Away." The Yasawa Islands, with their dramatic volcanic landscapes and secluded bays, provide a more remote and tranquil experience. Sailing through these islands allows you to anchor in pristine lagoons, snorkel in coral gardens, and visit traditional Fijian villages.

Another prime sailing destination in Fiji is the Lau Group, located to the east of the main islands. The Lau Islands are less frequented by tourists, offering a more off-the-beaten-path adventure. These islands are known for their untouched beauty, with lush greenery, limestone cliffs, and crystal-clear waters. The Lau Group offers a unique blend of Polynesian and Melanesian cultures, providing an enriching cultural experience. Sailing through the Lau Islands allows you to explore hidden coves, discover ancient archaeological sites, and experience traditional Fijian hospitality. The remoteness and unspoiled nature of the Lau Group make it a dream destination for adventurous sailors looking to explore the lesser-known parts of Fiji.

For those seeking a mix of adventure and luxury, the northern islands of Vanua Levu and Taveuni offer a perfect sailing itinerary. Vanua Levu, the second-largest island in Fiji, is known for its lush rainforests, hot springs, and vibrant coral reefs. Savusavu, a picturesque town on the southern coast of Vanua Levu, is a popular port of call for yachts and offers excellent facilities for sailors. The town is surrounded by beautiful anchorages, making it an ideal base for exploring the island's natural wonders. Taveuni, also known as the "Garden Island," is famous for its waterfalls, lush landscapes, and rich marine biodiversity. Sailing around Taveuni provides opportunities for snorkeling and diving in some of Fiji's most pristine waters, including the famous Rainbow Reef.

The Viti Levu Bay area, located on the main island's northern coast, is another excellent sailing destination. This region offers a mix of tranquil anchorages, vibrant coral reefs, and traditional Fijian villages. Sailing through Viti Levu Bay allows you to explore the beautiful Nananu-i-Ra Island, known for its white sandy beaches and excellent windsurfing conditions. The bay also provides access to the

Bligh Water, a renowned diving area famous for its dramatic underwater landscapes and diverse marine life. The combination of serene anchorages and world-class diving makes Viti Levu Bay a must-visit for sailing enthusiasts.

One of the unique aspects of sailing in Fiji is the opportunity to experience the traditional Fijian way of life. Many sailing itineraries include visits to local villages, where you can participate in cultural ceremonies, learn about traditional crafts, and enjoy authentic Fijian hospitality. The kava ceremony, a traditional ritual involving the preparation and drinking of kava, is a highlight of any village visit. This ceremony is a symbol of unity and respect, offering a chance to connect with the local community. Sailing provides a unique vantage point to access these remote villages and experience Fijian culture in a way that is not possible through conventional travel.

Fiji's favorable sailing conditions are another significant draw for maritime enthusiasts. The trade winds, which blow from the southeast, provide consistent and steady breezes ideal for sailing. The warm tropical climate ensures pleasant sailing conditions year-round, with the dry season from May to October being the most popular time for sailing. During this period, the weather is cooler, and the seas are calmer, making it ideal for exploring the islands. The wet season, from November to April, brings warmer temperatures and occasional tropical storms, but it is also a time when the islands are lush and vibrant. Regardless of the season, Fiji's waters offer excellent visibility, making it perfect for snorkeling and diving.

Fiji's well-established yachting infrastructure further enhances the sailing experience. The country has several marinas and yacht clubs that provide a range of services and facilities for sailors. The Port Denarau Marina, located near Nadi, is one of the largest and most well-equipped marinas in Fiji. It offers a full range of services, including refueling, provisioning, maintenance, and repair facilities. The marina is also a gateway to the Mamanuca and Yasawa Islands, making it a convenient starting point for sailing adventures. Other notable marinas include the Vuda Marina near Lautoka, the Copra Shed Marina in Savusavu, and the Royal Suva Yacht Club in Suva. These marinas provide safe and secure mooring options, making it easy for sailors to explore the islands at their own pace.

Chartering a yacht in Fiji is a popular option for those who do not have their own vessel. Several charter companies offer a range of yachts, from bareboat charters for experienced sailors to fully crewed yachts for those seeking a more relaxed and luxurious experience. Chartering a yacht allows you to explore Fiji's islands at your own pace, with the flexibility to choose your itinerary and activities. Whether you prefer a leisurely sail through calm waters, an adventurous voyage to remote islands, or a combination of both, chartering a yacht in Fiji provides the ultimate freedom and flexibility.

In addition to the natural beauty and cultural experiences, sailing in Fiji offers a wide range of water-based activities. Snorkeling and diving are among the most popular activities, with the coral reefs around the islands offering some of the best underwater experiences in the world. The vibrant marine life, including colorful reef fish, turtles, rays, and sharks, provides endless opportunities for exploration and discovery. Many sailing itineraries include stops at renowned dive sites, allowing you to experience the underwater wonders of Fiji.

Fishing is another popular activity for sailors in Fiji. The warm waters are home to a variety of fish species, including tuna, mahi-mahi, wahoo, and marlin. Whether you prefer deep-sea fishing or casting a line from your yacht, Fiji's waters offer excellent fishing opportunities. Some charter companies also provide fishing gear and experienced guides to enhance your fishing experience.

For those seeking relaxation, the tranquil anchorages and secluded beaches provide the perfect setting for unwinding and enjoying the natural beauty of the islands. Whether you prefer sunbathing on the deck of your yacht, enjoying a picnic on a deserted beach, or simply soaking in the serene surroundings, sailing in Fiji offers a peaceful escape from the stresses of everyday life.

Kayaking and Paddleboarding

Fiji's stunning landscapes, clear waters, and tropical climate make it an ideal destination for water-based activities like kayaking and paddleboarding. These activities offer a unique way to explore Fiji's islands, coastlines, and marine ecosystems, providing both adventure and relaxation. and practical tips to make the most of your adventure.

Kayaking and paddleboarding in Fiji provide an intimate and immersive way to experience the country's natural beauty. Unlike larger watercraft, kayaks and paddleboards allow you to navigate shallow waters, explore hidden coves, and get up close to the vibrant marine life. Whether you are gliding over coral reefs, paddling through mangroves, or exploring secluded beaches, these activities offer a peaceful and environmentally friendly way to connect with nature.

One of the top destinations for kayaking and paddleboarding in Fiji is the Mamanuca Islands. Located west of Viti Levu, this group of islands is known for its clear turquoise waters, white sandy beaches, and vibrant coral reefs. The calm and sheltered waters around the Mamanuca Islands are perfect for beginners and experienced paddlers alike. You can rent a kayak or paddleboard from one of the many resorts or tour operators in the area and set off to explore the stunning coastline. Highlights include paddling around Malolo Island, where you can enjoy views of the lush interior and pristine beaches, and exploring the coral reefs around Mana Island, where you can see colorful fish, rays, and even turtles.

The Yasawa Islands, located further north of the Mamanucas, offer another fantastic destination for kayaking and paddleboarding. The Yasawas are known for their dramatic landscapes, including volcanic peaks, limestone cliffs, and secluded bays. The crystal-clear waters and diverse marine life make the Yasawa Islands a paradise for paddlers. One popular route is to paddle from Nanuya Lailai Island to the nearby Blue Lagoon, where you can enjoy the calm, shallow waters and explore the coral reefs. Another great spot is Sawa-i-Lau, where you can paddle through limestone caves and enjoy the stunning scenery. The remote and unspoiled nature of the Yasawa Islands provides a sense of adventure and discovery, making it a memorable kayaking and paddleboarding destination.

Vanua Levu, Fiji's second-largest island, offers a more off-the-beaten-path experience for paddlers. The island's diverse coastline includes mangrove forests, coral reefs, and quiet bays, providing a variety of environments to explore. Savusavu Bay, located on the southern coast of Vanua Levu, is a popular spot for kayaking and paddleboarding. The bay is sheltered and calm, making it ideal for paddling. You can explore the mangroves, paddle along the coastline, and even visit the nearby hot springs. Another great spot on Vanua Levu is Natewa Bay, the largest bay in the South Pacific. Natewa Bay is known for its rich marine biodiversity, including dolphins, whales, and a variety of fish species. Paddling through Natewa Bay offers a unique opportunity to see these animals in their natural habitat and enjoy the stunning coastal scenery.

The island of Taveuni, also known as the "Garden Island," is another excellent destination for kayaking and paddleboarding. Taveuni is famous for its lush rainforests, waterfalls, and coral reefs. One of the best spots for paddling on Taveuni is the Somosomo Strait, located between Taveuni and Vanua Levu. The strait is home to the famous Rainbow Reef, known for its vibrant soft corals and diverse marine life. Paddling through the Somosomo Strait allows you to see the coral reefs up close and enjoy the clear waters and stunning underwater scenery. Another great spot on Taveuni is the Bouma National Heritage Park, where you can paddle along the coastline and explore the park's beaches, waterfalls, and rainforests.

The Coral Coast, located on the southern coast of Viti Levu, offers a variety of paddling experiences. The Coral Coast is known for its fringing reefs, white sandy beaches, and clear waters. One popular spot is the Sigatoka River, where you can paddle through the river's mangroves and enjoy the lush vegetation and wildlife. Another great spot on the Coral Coast is the area around the town of Pacific Harbour, known as the "Adventure Capital of Fiji." Here, you can paddle along the coastline, explore the coral reefs, and even try paddleboarding in the surf. The Coral Coast offers a mix of calm waters and more challenging conditions, making it suitable for paddlers of all levels.

For those looking for a more remote and adventurous paddling experience, the Lau Islands offer a unique opportunity to explore one of the most unspoiled parts of Fiji. The Lau Islands are located to the east of the main islands and are known for their pristine beauty and rich cultural heritage. Paddling through the Lau Islands allows you to explore hidden coves, limestone cliffs, and coral reefs. The islands are less visited by tourists, providing a sense of solitude and adventure. Highlights include paddling around Fulaga Island, known for its stunning lagoon and limestone formations, and exploring the coral reefs around Lakeba Island. The Lau Islands offer a true sense of exploration and discovery, making it a perfect destination for adventurous paddlers.

In addition to these top spots, there are many other beautiful and diverse locations in Fiji that are perfect for kayaking and paddleboarding. The islands of Kadavu, Beqa, and Ovalau all offer unique paddling experiences, with their own distinct landscapes and marine environments. Each location provides a different perspective on Fiji's natural beauty and offers a variety of paddling opportunities.

When planning a kayaking or paddleboarding adventure in Fiji, there are a few practical considerations to keep in mind. First, it's important to choose the right equipment. Most resorts and tour operators in Fiji offer kayak and paddleboard rentals, and some even provide guided tours. It's a good idea to check the condition of the equipment and ensure that it is suitable for your skill level. If you're new to kayaking or paddleboarding, consider taking a lesson or joining a guided tour to get started.

Safety is also a key consideration. Always wear a life jacket and be aware of the weather conditions and tides. It's important to stay hydrated and protect yourself from the sun by wearing sunscreen, a hat, and protective clothing. If you're paddling in a remote area, let someone know your plans and carry a communication device in case of emergency.

Respect for the environment is another important aspect of kayaking and paddleboarding in Fiji. The country's marine ecosystems are delicate and need to be protected. Avoid touching or disturbing the coral reefs and marine life, and be mindful of your impact on the environment. Many areas in Fiji are protected marine reserves, and it's important to follow local regulations and guidelines to help preserve these beautiful environments for future generations.

Deep-Sea Fishing Excursions

Deep-sea fishing in Fiji offers an unparalleled adventure for both seasoned anglers and novices alike. The rich and diverse marine environment, combined with the stunning natural beauty of the islands, makes Fiji one of the premier destinations for deep-sea fishing excursions.

Fiji's location in the heart of the South Pacific means it is surrounded by deep, nutrient-rich waters that support a wide variety of marine life. This abundance makes Fiji an ideal place for deep-sea fishing, where the thrill of the catch is matched by the beauty of the surroundings. The islands are situated in an area where the warm tropical waters meet deeper, cooler currents, creating perfect conditions for a variety of fish species to thrive.

One of the most popular areas for deep-sea fishing in Fiji is the waters surrounding Viti Levu, the largest island in the archipelago. The Coral Coast, located on the southern coast of Viti Levu, is particularly renowned for its excellent fishing opportunities. Here, anglers can expect to catch a variety of game fish, including yellowfin tuna, mahi-mahi (dolphinfish), wahoo, and marlin. The deep waters just off the coast provide the perfect hunting grounds for these fast and powerful fish. Chartering a fishing boat from one of the many operators along the Coral Coast is a straightforward process, and these charters often include experienced guides who know the best spots and techniques for a successful fishing trip.

The northern waters around Vanua Levu, Fiji's second-largest island, are also prime locations for deep-sea fishing. Savusavu, a quaint town on the southern coast of Vanua Levu, serves as a popular base for fishing excursions. The waters around Savusavu are known for their rich biodiversity and the presence of large pelagic species. Anglers can expect to encounter sailfish, giant trevally, and barracuda, among other species. The area is also famous for its underwater seamounts and drop-offs, which attract a variety of fish and create an exciting environment for deep-sea fishing.

The waters off the Yasawa and Mamanuca Islands offer another fantastic deep-sea fishing destination. These islands are not only famous for their stunning beaches and clear waters but also for their abundant marine life. The deep channels between the islands are prime spots for catching big game fish such as marlin, swordfish, and tuna. The combination of scenic island views and the thrill of reeling in a big catch makes fishing in the Yasawa and Mamanuca Islands a truly unforgettable experience. Many resorts in these islands offer fishing charters as part of their activity packages, making it easy for visitors to enjoy a day out on the water.

Kadavu Island, located south of Viti Levu, is another excellent destination for deep-sea fishing. Kadavu is surrounded by the Great Astrolabe Reef, one of the largest barrier reefs in the world. The deep waters around the reef are home to a variety of large game fish, including marlin, sailfish, and mahi-mahi. The island's remote location means that the waters are less crowded, providing a more peaceful and solitary fishing experience. The local fishing guides on Kadavu have extensive knowledge of the area and can take anglers to the best spots for a successful catch.

When it comes to the types of fish you can expect to catch in Fiji, the variety is impressive. Yellowfin tuna are one of the most sought-after species, known for their size, strength, and speed. These fish can weigh over 200 pounds and provide a thrilling challenge for anglers. Mahi-mahi, with their striking colors and acrobatic leaps, are another popular catch. Wahoo, known for their incredible speed and razor-sharp teeth, are also abundant in Fiji's waters. Marlin, including blue, black, and striped varieties, are the ultimate prize for many deep-sea fishermen, with their size and power making for an exhilarating battle.

Giant trevally, or GTs, are another prized catch in Fiji. These powerful fish are known for their aggressive strikes and fighting ability. They can be found around reefs, drop-offs, and inshore waters, providing a diverse range of fishing opportunities. Sailfish, with their distinctive dorsal fins and rapid bursts of speed, are also a common target for anglers in Fiji. Their spectacular leaps and acrobatics make them a thrilling catch.

Barracuda, with their long, slender bodies and sharp teeth, are another species commonly encountered in Fiji's waters. These predatory fish are known for their speed and agility, making them a challenging and exciting catch. Fiji's diverse marine environment means that anglers can also encounter a variety of other species, including snapper, grouper, and various types of reef fish.

A typical deep-sea fishing excursion in Fiji begins early in the morning, with anglers boarding a chartered fishing boat equipped with all the necessary gear and equipment. The experienced crew and guides will provide instruction and assistance, ensuring that even novice anglers can enjoy a successful fishing trip. The boat will head out to the deeper waters, where the crew will use their knowledge of the local conditions and fish behavior to locate the best fishing spots.

Once a suitable location is reached, the crew will set up the fishing lines and begin trolling for fish. Trolling involves dragging baited lines behind the boat at various depths, enticing the fish to strike. This method is particularly effective for catching large pelagic species such as marlin, tuna, and wahoo. The excitement begins when a fish takes the bait, and the angler must use skill and strength to reel in the catch. The crew will provide guidance and support throughout the process, ensuring that the fish is safely landed.

In addition to trolling, other fishing techniques such as jigging, popping, and live bait fishing can be used depending on the target species and conditions. Jigging involves dropping a weighted lure to the bottom and rapidly retrieving it to attract fish. Popping uses surface lures that create a commotion on the water's surface, enticing fish to strike. Live bait fishing involves using live fish or other natural bait to attract larger predators. Each technique requires different skills and equipment, adding variety and excitement to the fishing experience.

Deep-sea fishing in Fiji is not only about the thrill of the catch but also about enjoying the natural beauty and tranquility of the open ocean. The clear, blue waters and stunning island views create a serene and picturesque backdrop for the adventure. The chance to see dolphins, whales, and seabirds adds to the experience, making each trip unique and memorable.

For those looking to combine deep-sea fishing with luxury and relaxation, many resorts in Fiji offer exclusive fishing packages that include accommodation, meals, and guided fishing trips. These packages often feature top-of-the-line boats and equipment, as well as personalized service and attention to detail. Anglers can enjoy a day of fishing followed by a relaxing evening at the resort, complete with gourmet dining and spa treatments.

Conservation is an important aspect of deep-sea fishing in Fiji. Many charter operators and resorts follow sustainable fishing practices to ensure the health and longevity of the marine environment. Catch and release is a common practice for certain species, allowing fish to be returned to the water unharmed. By following ethical and sustainable fishing practices, anglers can help preserve Fiji's rich marine biodiversity for future generations.

CHAPTER 9

LAND ADVENTURES AND NATURE

Hiking Trails and Nature Walks

Exploring the hiking trails and nature walks in Fiji offers an incredible opportunity to immerse yourself in the country's stunning landscapes and rich biodiversity. From lush rainforests and cascading waterfalls to volcanic mountains and coastal mangroves, Fiji's diverse terrain provides a wide range of hiking experiences suitable for all levels of fitness and adventure.

Fiji's main island, Viti Levu, is home to some of the most accessible and varied hiking trails in the country. One of the most popular trails is the Sigatoka Sand Dunes National Park, located on the Coral Coast. This park is Fiji's first national park and is renowned for its striking sand dunes, which range in height from 20 to 60 meters. The park offers several walking trails that wind through coastal forest, grasslands, and along the dunes themselves. As you hike, you can enjoy panoramic views of the ocean and explore archaeological sites where ancient artifacts have been discovered. The park is also home to a variety of bird species, making it a great spot for birdwatching.

Another fantastic hiking destination on Viti Levu is the Colo-i-Suva Forest Park, located near Suva. This lush rainforest park offers a network of well-maintained trails that lead you through dense forest, past clear freshwater pools, and to several picturesque waterfalls. The park is a haven for nature lovers, with its rich biodiversity and serene environment. As you hike, you may encounter various bird species, butterflies, and other wildlife. The cool, shaded trails and the opportunity to swim in the natural pools make this a refreshing and enjoyable hike, especially on a hot day.

For a more challenging hike, consider tackling Mount Tomanivi, the highest peak in Fiji. Located in the northern part of Viti Levu, this dormant volcano rises to an elevation of 1,324 meters. The hike to the summit of Mount Tomanivi is a strenuous trek that takes you through montane forest and offers stunning views of the surrounding landscape. On a clear day, you can see as far as the Yasawa and Mamanuca Islands from the summit. The trail is steep and can be slippery, so it is recommended for experienced hikers. Reaching the top of Mount Tomanivi is a rewarding accomplishment and provides a unique perspective on Fiji's geography.

On the island of Taveuni, often referred to as the "Garden Island" of Fiji, you will find some of the country's most scenic hiking trails. The Bouma National Heritage Park is a must-visit destination for hikers. This park covers over 150 square kilometers and is known for its lush rainforest, dramatic waterfalls, and diverse flora and fauna. One of the most popular hikes in the park is the Lavena Coastal Walk, a beautiful trail that follows the coastline through traditional

Fijian villages, across rivers, and along pristine beaches. The trail ends at a stunning waterfall where you can take a refreshing swim. The Lavena Coastal Walk is relatively easy and can be enjoyed by hikers of all ages.

Another highlight in the Bouma National Heritage Park is the Tavoro Waterfalls. The hike to the waterfalls is relatively short but offers a rewarding experience. The trail takes you through dense rainforest to three cascading waterfalls, each with its own swimming pool. The first waterfall is easily accessible and is a popular spot for a swim. The second and third waterfalls require a bit more effort to reach but offer a more secluded and tranquil experience. The natural beauty and serenity of the Tavoro Waterfalls make this hike a favorite among visitors to Taveuni.

Vanua Levu, Fiji's second-largest island, also offers excellent hiking opportunities. The Waisali Rainforest Reserve, located near Savusavu, is a protected area that provides a glimpse into the island's pristine rainforest. The reserve features a well-maintained trail that takes you through lush vegetation, past clear streams, and to a picturesque waterfall. Along the way, you can observe a variety of plant and animal species, including orchids, ferns, and birds. The Waisali Rainforest Reserve is a great destination for nature lovers and offers a peaceful and immersive hiking experience.

The island of Kadavu, located south of Viti Levu, is known for its rugged terrain and rich biodiversity. The hiking trails on Kadavu offer a more remote and adventurous experience. One of the best hikes on the island is the trek to the Kadavu Island's highest peak, Mount Washington. The trail takes you through dense forest, along ridges, and to the summit, where you can enjoy panoramic views of the island and the surrounding ocean. The hike is challenging and requires a good level of fitness, but the stunning scenery and sense of accomplishment make it well worth the effort.

Fiji's smaller islands also offer some fantastic hiking opportunities. On the island of Ovalau, you can explore the historic town of Levuka and its surrounding hills. Levuka, Fiji's former capital, is a UNESCO World Heritage Site known for its colonial architecture and historical significance. The hiking trails around Levuka take you through lush forest, past old plantations, and to viewpoints that offer stunning vistas of the town and the ocean. The combination of history, culture, and natural beauty makes hiking on Ovalau a unique and enriching experience.

The Mamanuca and Yasawa Islands, known for their stunning beaches and clear waters, also offer some great hiking experiences. On Malolo Island in the Mamanucas, you can hike to the island's highest point, Malolo Lookout. The trail takes you through tropical vegetation and offers breathtaking views of the surrounding islands and ocean. The hike is relatively short but steep, making it a rewarding challenge. In the Yasawas, you can explore the hills and ridges of the islands, with trails that offer panoramic views of the archipelago. The combination of coastal scenery and island landscapes makes hiking in the Mamanucas and Yasawas a memorable experience.

For those interested in a guided hiking experience, many resorts and tour operators in Fiji offer guided hikes and nature walks. These guided tours provide valuable insights into the local flora and fauna, as well as the cultural and historical significance of the areas you are exploring. Knowledgeable guides can enhance your hiking experience by sharing their expertise and pointing out interesting features along the way.

When planning a hiking trip in Fiji, it is important to consider the weather and trail conditions. The dry season, from May to October, is generally the best time for hiking, as the weather is cooler and the trails are less muddy. The wet season, from November to April, can bring heavy rains and higher temperatures, making some trails more challenging and less accessible. It is also important to wear appropriate clothing and footwear, carry plenty of water, and be prepared for the tropical climate.

Bird Watching and Wildlife Tours

Bird watching and wildlife tours in Fiji offer a unique and enriching experience for nature enthusiasts, allowing them to explore the islands' rich biodiversity and stunning natural landscapes. Fiji's diverse ecosystems, ranging from lush rainforests and mangroves to coral reefs and coastal wetlands, provide a habitat for a wide variety of bird species and other wildlife. This detailed explanation will provide an extensive overview of bird watching and wildlife tours in Fiji, highlighting the key locations, species you can expect to see, and the overall experience of exploring Fiji's natural beauty.

Fiji is home to over 160 species of birds, including 27 endemic species that are found nowhere else in the world. This makes Fiji a prime destination for bird watchers looking to see unique and rare species. The islands' varied habitats support a rich diversity of birdlife, from colorful parrots and vibrant kingfishers to majestic seabirds and elusive forest dwellers.

One of the best locations for bird watching in Fiji is the island of Taveuni, often referred to as the "Garden Island" due to its lush vegetation and abundant wildlife. Taveuni's diverse habitats, including rainforests, mangroves, and coastal areas, make it a haven for birdlife. The Bouma National Heritage Park on Taveuni is a prime spot for bird watching. This park covers over 150 square kilometers and includes a variety of ecosystems that support numerous bird species. Some of the key species you can expect to see in Bouma National Heritage Park include the orange dove, the silktail, and the Fiji goshawk. The orange dove, with its bright orange plumage, is one of Fiji's most striking birds and is found only on Taveuni and a few other islands. The silktail, another endemic species, is a small bird with glossy black plumage and white tail feathers, and it inhabits the dense undergrowth of the forest. The Fiji goshawk, a medium-sized raptor, is often seen perched in the treetops or soaring overhead.

Another excellent bird watching destination in Fiji is the island of Viti Levu, the largest island in the archipelago. Viti Levu offers a range of habitats that support a diverse array of bird species. The Colo-i-Suva Forest Park, located near Suva, is a popular spot for bird watching. This lush rainforest park is home to many native bird species, including the collared lory, the masked shining parrot, and the red-vented bulbul. The collared lory, with its bright red and green plumage, is often seen feeding on nectar and fruits in the treetops. The masked shining parrot, a colorful and vocal bird, is found in the forest canopy and is known for its striking appearance and loud calls. The red-vented bulbul, an introduced species, is commonly seen in gardens and forest edges.

The Sigatoka Sand Dunes National Park, located on the Coral Coast of Viti Levu, is another great spot for bird watching. The park's unique dune ecosystem supports a variety of bird species, including the Fiji bush warbler, the Pacific golden plover, and the Fiji parrotfinch. The Fiji bush warbler is a small, brown bird that is often seen flitting through the undergrowth, while the Pacific golden plover is a migratory shorebird that can be found along the coast during certain times of the year. The Fiji parrotfinch, with its bright green plumage and red head, is a striking and colorful bird that is often seen in the park's grasslands and scrub areas.

Vanua Levu, Fiji's second-largest island, also offers excellent bird watching opportunities. The Waisali Rainforest Reserve, located near Savusavu, is a protected area that provides a glimpse into the island's pristine rainforest. The reserve is home to many bird species, including the Vanikoro flycatcher, the wattled honeyeater, and the silktail. The Vanikoro flycatcher is a small, insectivorous bird with a distinctive white eye-ring and black plumage, while the wattled honeyeater is a medium-sized bird with a yellow face and throat and is often seen feeding on nectar and insects. The silktail, also found on Taveuni, can be spotted in the dense undergrowth of the Waisali Rainforest Reserve.

The island of Kadavu, located south of Viti Levu, is another excellent destination for bird watching. Kadavu is home to several endemic bird species, including the Kadavu parrot, the Kadavu honeyeater, and the Kadavu fantail. The Kadavu parrot, with its bright green and red plumage, is one of the island's most striking birds and is often seen in the forest canopy. The Kadavu honeyeater, a medium-sized bird with a distinctive yellow throat and face, is found in the island's forests and coastal areas. The Kadavu fantail, a small, active bird with a fan-shaped tail, is often seen flitting through the undergrowth in search of insects.

In addition to bird watching, Fiji offers a variety of wildlife tours that allow visitors to explore the islands' diverse ecosystems and encounter a range of animal species. The marine environment around Fiji is particularly rich in biodiversity, with coral reefs, mangroves, and seagrass beds providing habitat for a wide variety of marine life. Snorkeling and diving tours offer the chance to see colorful reef fish, sea turtles, sharks, and rays in their natural habitat. The Great Astrolabe Reef, located off the coast of Kadavu, is one of Fiji's premier diving destinations and offers the opportunity to see an incredible diversity of marine life.

For those interested in terrestrial wildlife, Fiji's forests and wetlands are home to a variety of reptiles, amphibians, and mammals. The crested iguana, an endemic species found only on a few islands in Fiji, is one of the country's most unique reptiles. These iguanas are characterized by their bright green coloration and distinctive crest along their back. They can be found in the dry forests and coastal areas of islands such as Yadua Taba and Monuriki. The Fiji banded iguana, another endemic species, is found in the rainforests of the larger islands and is known for its striking black and green bands.

Fiji's wetlands and mangroves are also important habitats for a variety of wildlife. The Rewa Delta, located on the eastern coast of Viti Levu, is one of the largest wetland areas in Fiji and provides habitat for a range of bird species, fish, and invertebrates. Guided boat tours through the mangroves offer the chance to see herons, kingfishers, and mudskippers, as well as the occasional saltwater crocodile.

For a truly unique wildlife experience, consider visiting one of Fiji's marine protected areas, such as the Namena Marine

Reserve or the Vatu-i-Ra Conservation Park. These areas are home to some of the healthiest and most diverse coral reefs in the world and offer the opportunity to see a wide variety of marine life. Snorkeling and diving tours in these reserves provide a glimpse into the underwater world of Fiji, with its colorful coral gardens, schools of fish, and larger pelagic species.

When planning a bird watching or wildlife tour in Fiji, it is important to consider the best times of year to visit. The dry season, from May to October, is generally the best time for bird watching and wildlife tours, as the weather is cooler and the chances of rain are lower. The wet season, from November to April, can bring heavy rains and higher temperatures, but it is also a time when many bird species are more active and visible.

It is also important to respect the environment and practice responsible wildlife viewing. This includes staying on designated trails, keeping a safe distance from animals, and avoiding disturbing their natural behavior. Many tour operators in Fiji follow sustainable and ethical practices to minimize their impact on the environment and support local conservation efforts.

Visiting Fiji's National Parks

Visiting Fiji's national parks offers an extraordinary opportunity to explore the country's rich natural heritage, diverse ecosystems, and stunning landscapes. Fiji is home to several national parks, each showcasing unique features and offering a range of activities for nature lovers, adventurers, and those seeking tranquility.

One of the most prominent national parks in Fiji is the Bouma National Heritage Park on the island of Taveuni. Known as the "Garden Island" of Fiji, Taveuni boasts lush rainforests, pristine waterfalls, and diverse wildlife. The Bouma National Heritage Park, covering over 150 square kilometers, is a prime example of Taveuni's natural beauty and ecological richness. Established in 1990, the park was created to protect the island's rainforest and to provide sustainable livelihoods for the local communities through eco-tourism.

The park is divided into several sections, each offering unique attractions and experiences. One of the most popular areas is the Tavoro Waterfalls, a series of three stunning waterfalls set amidst dense rainforest. The first waterfall, known as the Lower Tavoro Waterfall, is easily accessible and features a large pool at its base, perfect for swimming. A moderate hike through the rainforest leads to the second and third waterfalls, which are more secluded and offer a tranquil and refreshing experience. The trails are well-maintained and provide opportunities to observe the rich biodiversity of the area, including various bird species, insects, and plant life.

Another highlight of Bouma National Heritage Park is the Lavena Coastal Walk. This scenic trail follows the coastline through traditional Fijian villages, lush rainforest, and along pristine beaches. The walk offers stunning views of the ocean, waterfalls, and the surrounding landscape. The trail ends at the beautiful Lavena Waterfall, where visitors can take a refreshing swim in the natural pool. The Lavena Coastal Walk is relatively easy and suitable for all ages, making it a popular activity for families and nature enthusiasts.

In addition to the natural beauty, Bouma National Heritage Park is also significant for its cultural heritage. The local communities play an active role in managing the park and benefit from eco-tourism initiatives. Visitors can experience Fijian culture and hospitality by participating in village tours, traditional ceremonies, and handicraft demonstrations. This integration of nature and culture makes a visit to Bouma National Heritage Park a truly enriching experience.

Another notable national park in Fiji is the Sigatoka Sand Dunes National Park, located on the Coral Coast of Viti Levu. Established in 1989, this park is Fiji's first national park and is renowned for its unique sand dune ecosystem. The park covers an area of approximately 650 hectares and features dunes that range in height from 20 to 60 meters. The Sigatoka Sand Dunes are formed from river and ocean sediments and have been shaped by wind and waves over thousands of years.

The park offers several walking trails that allow visitors to explore the diverse landscapes, including coastal forest, grasslands, and the dunes themselves. One of the trails leads to an archaeological site where ancient artifacts, pottery, and human remains have been discovered, providing insights into Fiji's early inhabitants. The Sigatoka Sand Dunes are also an important habitat for various bird species, including the Pacific golden plover, the Fiji bush warbler, and the Fiji parrotfinch. Bird watchers will enjoy the opportunity to observe these species in their natural environment.

The park's visitor center provides information about the geology, ecology, and cultural history of the area. Guided tours are available, offering deeper insights into the significance of the dunes and the surrounding ecosystem. The combination of natural beauty, archaeological significance, and rich biodiversity makes the Sigatoka Sand Dunes National Park a must-visit destination for those interested in Fiji's natural and cultural heritage.

The Colo-i-Suva Forest Park, located near Suva on Viti Levu, is another excellent destination for nature enthusiasts. This lush rainforest park covers an area of approximately 2.5 square kilometers and offers a network of well-maintained trails that wind through dense forest, past clear freshwater pools, and to several picturesque waterfalls. The park is a haven for bird watchers, with many native bird species, including the collared lory, the masked shining parrot, and the Fiji goshawk.

One of the highlights of Colo-i-Suva Forest Park is the series of natural swimming holes formed by the Waisila Creek.

These pools are fed by small waterfalls and offer a refreshing escape from the tropical heat. The trails in the park vary in difficulty, making it accessible for both casual walkers and more experienced hikers. The park's serene environment and rich biodiversity make it a popular spot for picnicking, bird watching, and nature walks.

For those interested in marine conservation, the Namena Marine Reserve is a must-visit destination. Located off the coast of Vanua Levu, this marine protected area covers approximately 70 square kilometers and is home to some of the healthiest and most diverse coral reefs in the world. The reserve was established to protect the rich marine biodiversity and to promote sustainable fishing practices.

The Namena Marine Reserve offers some of the best snorkeling and diving experiences in Fiji. The clear waters and vibrant coral gardens are teeming with marine life, including colorful reef fish, sea turtles, sharks, and rays. Divers can explore underwater pinnacles, walls, and drop-offs, each offering unique and breathtaking views of the marine ecosystem. The reserve is also a critical breeding ground for various fish species, making it an important area for marine conservation.

Visitors to the Namena Marine Reserve can also learn about the local conservation efforts and the importance of protecting marine environments. The reserve is managed in partnership with the local communities, who play a vital role in its preservation. This collaboration ensures that the benefits of eco-tourism are shared with the local people, promoting sustainable development and environmental stewardship.

The Koroyanitu National Heritage Park, located on the western side of Viti Levu, is another significant natural area in Fiji. The park covers an area of approximately 35 square kilometers and includes several traditional villages, montane forest, and grasslands. One of the main attractions of the park is Mount Batilamu, also known as "Sleeping Giant," which offers panoramic views of the surrounding landscape.

Hiking to the summit of Mount Batilamu is a rewarding experience that takes you through diverse habitats, including tropical forest and grassy ridges. The trail is well-marked and provides opportunities to see a variety of plant and animal species, including orchids, ferns, and birds. The summit offers stunning views of the Yasawa Islands, Nadi Bay, and the interior of Viti Levu.

The park also offers cultural experiences, with guided tours available in the traditional villages. Visitors can learn about Fijian customs, participate in traditional ceremonies, and experience the hospitality of the local communities. The integration of natural beauty and cultural heritage makes the Koroyanitu National Heritage Park a unique and enriching destination.

Another noteworthy national park is the Sovi Basin Protected Area, located in the central highlands of Viti Levu.

The Sovi Basin is one of the largest remaining tracts of undisturbed rainforest in Fiji and is home to a rich diversity of flora and fauna. The area is a key conservation site and provides habitat for many endangered and endemic species.

Exploring the Sovi Basin offers a chance to experience Fiji's pristine rainforest and its incredible biodiversity. The area is characterized by rugged terrain, deep valleys, and numerous rivers and streams. Guided tours are available, offering insights into the ecological significance of the basin and the efforts being made to protect it. The Sovi Basin is also an important cultural site, with several traditional villages located within the protected area.

Exploring Caves and Waterfalls

Exploring caves and waterfalls in Fiji offers an enchanting glimpse into the country's natural beauty and geological diversity. The archipelago's dramatic landscapes are dotted with numerous caves and cascading waterfalls, each with its own unique features and stories.

Fiji's caves are remarkable both for their natural formations and their cultural significance. One of the most famous caves is the Sawa-i-Lau Caves, located in the Yasawa Islands. These limestone caves are renowned for their stunning rock formations and crystal-clear blue waters. According to local legend, the caves are the resting place of the ancient Fijian god Ulutini. The main cave is easily accessible and features a large chamber with a natural skylight that illuminates the interior, creating a magical atmosphere. Adventurous visitors can swim through an underwater tunnel to reach a second, hidden chamber, which adds an element of excitement to the exploration. The Sawa-i-Lau Caves are not only a natural wonder but also a site of historical and cultural importance, offering a unique blend of adventure and heritage.

Another notable cave system in Fiji is the Naihehe Cave, located in the Sigatoka Valley on Viti Levu. Naihehe, meaning "a place to get lost," is the largest cave system in Fiji and was historically used as a fortress by the ancient Fijian tribes. Visitors can explore the cave's vast chambers, which are adorned with impressive stalactites and stalagmites. The cave also contains a sacred burial site, adding to its historical significance. The journey to Naihehe Cave often involves a guided tour that includes a scenic drive through the Sigatoka Valley and a river crossing, making the adventure even more immersive. Inside the cave, visitors can learn about its history and the way it was used as a refuge during times of conflict.

In addition to caves, Fiji is renowned for its breathtaking waterfalls, which are scattered across its islands. One of the most famous waterfalls is the Tavoro Waterfalls, located in the Bouma National Heritage Park on Taveuni. The Tavoro Waterfalls consist of three cascades, each with its own unique charm. The first waterfall, known as the Lower Tavoro Waterfall, is easily accessible and features a large pool at its base, perfect for swimming. The second and third waterfalls require a moderate hike through lush rainforest but offer more secluded and tranquil settings. The trails to the waterfalls are well-maintained and provide opportunities to observe the rich biodiversity of the area, including various bird species, insects, and plant life. The Tavoro Waterfalls are a must-visit destination for anyone looking to experience the natural beauty and serenity of Taveuni.

Another stunning waterfall on Taveuni is the Bouma Falls, also located within the Bouma National Heritage Park. The Bouma Falls, also known as the Bouma Falls Trilogy, consist of three separate waterfalls, each offering its own unique experience. The first waterfall is easily accessible and features a large swimming pool at its base. The second and third waterfalls require a more strenuous hike but reward visitors with spectacular views and a more secluded setting. The Bouma Falls are surrounded by lush rainforest, making the hike to each waterfall an immersive experience in nature.

On the island of Vanua Levu, the Vuadomo Waterfall is a hidden gem that offers a peaceful and picturesque setting. Located near the village of Vuadomo, the waterfall is easily accessible and features a large pool at its base, ideal for swimming and relaxing. The surrounding area is lush and green, providing a serene backdrop for the waterfall. Visitors can take a short walk from the village to the waterfall, where they can enjoy the refreshing waters and the tranquil environment.

The island of Viti Levu also boasts several impressive waterfalls, including the Navua Gorge Waterfalls. Located in the interior of the island, the Navua Gorge is a stunning natural feature characterized by steep cliffs, dense rainforest, and cascading waterfalls. Visitors can take a guided tour that includes a boat ride up the Navua River, offering breathtaking views of the gorge and its waterfalls. The tour often includes opportunities to swim in the clear river waters and explore the surrounding rainforest. The Navua Gorge Waterfalls provide a unique and immersive experience in Fiji's natural beauty.

In the highlands of Viti Levu, the Savu-i-One Waterfall is another remarkable natural feature. Located near the village of Namosi, the Savu-i-One Waterfall is a tall, narrow cascade that plunges into a deep pool surrounded by lush vegetation. The hike to the waterfall takes visitors through rugged terrain and offers stunning views of the surrounding landscape. The pool at the base of the waterfall is perfect for swimming, and the remote location ensures a peaceful and secluded experience.

Fiji's waterfalls are not only beautiful but also play an important role in the local culture and ecosystem. Many of the waterfalls are considered sacred sites and are associated with local legends and traditions. The pristine waters of the waterfalls provide habitat for a variety of aquatic species and contribute to the overall health of the surrounding ecosystem. Visiting these natural wonders offers a chance to appreciate their beauty and significance while enjoying the serenity and tranquility they provide.

When planning a visit to Fiji's caves and waterfalls, it is important to consider the best times to visit and the necessary preparations. The dry season, from May to October, is generally the best time to explore these natural features, as the weather is cooler and the trails are less muddy. The wet season, from November to April, can bring heavy rains and higher water levels, making some areas more challenging to access.

It is also important to wear appropriate clothing and footwear, especially for hikes to remote waterfalls and caves. Comfortable, sturdy shoes with good grip are essential, as some trails can be steep and slippery. Bringing a swimsuit, towel, and plenty of water is also recommended, as many of the waterfalls offer opportunities for swimming and cooling off.

Guided tours are available for many of the caves and waterfalls in Fiji, offering valuable insights into their history, geology, and cultural significance. Local guides can enhance the experience by sharing their knowledge and ensuring the safety of the visitors. Respecting local customs and traditions is important, especially when visiting sites that are considered sacred by the local communities.

Zip-Lining and Canopy Tours

Zip-lining and canopy tours in Fiji offer thrilling and immersive experiences, allowing visitors to soar through lush rainforests, glide over river valleys, and take in the breathtaking views of the islands from above. These activities are perfect for adventure seekers and nature lovers alike, providing an exhilarating way to explore Fiji's stunning landscapes while enjoying the unique perspective that comes from high above the ground.

One of the most popular destinations for zip-lining in Fiji is located on the main island of Viti Levu, near the town of Pacific Harbour. Known as the "Adventure Capital of Fiji," Pacific Harbour is home to a renowned zip-lining course that takes you through the heart of the rainforest. This zip-lining experience features multiple lines that vary in length and speed, providing a range of thrills for participants. As you zip from platform to platform, you will soar over rivers, waterfalls, and dense forest canopy, with the chance to spot a variety of wildlife along the way. The course is designed to offer both excitement and safety, with experienced guides providing instruction and support throughout the tour.

The Pacific Harbour zip-lining adventure typically begins with a safety briefing and an introduction to the equipment. Participants are fitted with harnesses and helmets, and guides demonstrate the proper techniques for zip-lining. Once everyone is comfortable and ready, the adventure begins with a short hike to the first platform. From there, you will launch yourself off the platform and glide through the treetops, feeling the rush of wind and the thrill of speed as you travel from one line to the next. The zip-lining course offers a mix of short, fast lines and longer, scenic ones, allowing you to experience the beauty of the rainforest from different angles. Some lines even allow you to race side-by-side with a friend, adding an element of friendly competition to the adventure.

Another fantastic zip-lining destination in Fiji is located on the island of Taveuni. Known as the "Garden Island" of Fiji, Taveuni is renowned for its lush vegetation, stunning waterfalls, and rich biodiversity. The zip-lining course on Taveuni takes advantage of the island's natural beauty, offering a thrilling ride through the rainforest canopy. The course features multiple zip lines that traverse valleys and rivers, providing breathtaking views of the surrounding landscape. As you zip from one platform to the next, you can enjoy the sights and sounds of the rainforest, including the calls of native birds and the rustle of leaves in the breeze.

The Taveuni zip-lining experience is designed to be both exciting and accessible, with lines that cater to a range of skill levels. The course is built to international safety standards, and experienced guides are on hand to ensure that participants have a safe and enjoyable experience. Before starting the zip-lining adventure, participants receive a safety briefing and are fitted with the necessary equipment. The guides provide instruction on how to use the gear and demonstrate the proper techniques for zip-lining. Once everyone is ready, the adventure begins with a short hike to the first platform. From there, you will launch yourself into the air and glide through the treetops, experiencing the thrill of speed and the beauty of the rainforest from above.

For those looking for a unique zip-lining experience, the island of Vanua Levu offers an exciting option. Located near the town of Savusavu, the zip-lining course on Vanua Levu takes you through a stunning landscape of rolling hills, lush rainforest, and cascading waterfalls. The course features multiple zip lines that vary in length and speed, providing a range of thrills for participants. As you zip through the air, you can enjoy panoramic views of the surrounding landscape, including the sparkling waters of the Pacific Ocean and the distant mountains of Vanua Levu.

The Vanua Levu zip-lining experience begins with a safety briefing and an introduction to the equipment. Participants are fitted with harnesses and helmets, and guides demonstrate the proper techniques for zip-lining. Once everyone is comfortable and ready, the adventure begins with a hike to the first platform. From there, you will launch yourself off the platform and glide through the air, feeling the rush of wind and the thrill of speed as you travel from one line to the next. The course offers a mix of short, fast lines and longer, scenic ones, allowing you to experience the beauty of the landscape from different angles.

In addition to zip-lining, canopy tours offer another exciting way to explore Fiji's rainforests. Canopy tours involve navigating a series of elevated walkways, suspension bridges, and platforms built high in the treetops. These tours provide a unique perspective on the rainforest, allowing you to move through the canopy and observe the flora and fauna up close. Canopy tours are often combined with zip-lining, providing a comprehensive and immersive adventure in the treetops.

One of the best places for canopy tours in Fiji is the Colo-i-Suva Forest Park, located near Suva on Viti Levu. This lush rainforest park offers a network of trails, walkways, and platforms that allow you to explore the canopy and experience the beauty of the forest from above. The canopy tour takes you through dense vegetation, past clear freshwater pools, and to several picturesque waterfalls. The elevated walkways and suspension bridges provide stunning views of the forest and the chance to see a variety of bird species and other wildlife. The tour is designed to be both exciting and educational, with guides providing information about the rainforest ecosystem and the importance of conservation.

Another excellent destination for canopy tours is the Bouma National Heritage Park on Taveuni. This park is known for its lush rainforest, stunning waterfalls, and rich biodiversity, making it an ideal location for a canopy tour. The tour takes you through the treetops, offering breathtaking views of the forest and the chance to see a variety of plant and animal species up close. The elevated walkways and suspension bridges provide a unique perspective on the rainforest, allowing you to move through the canopy and observe the flora and fauna in their natural habitat. The tour is designed to be both thrilling and informative, with guides providing insights into the rainforest ecosystem and the importance of protecting these natural areas.

When planning a zip-lining or canopy tour adventure in Fiji, it is important to consider a few practical tips to ensure a safe and enjoyable experience. First, be sure to wear comfortable clothing and sturdy shoes with good grip. The terrain can be uneven and slippery, so appropriate footwear is essential. It is also a good idea to bring a hat, sunglasses, and sunscreen to protect yourself from the sun, as well as insect repellent to keep bugs at bay. Hydration is important, so bring plenty of water to stay hydrated throughout the tour.

Safety is a top priority on zip-lining and canopy tours, and it is important to follow the instructions provided by the guides. Pay attention during the safety briefing and ask questions if you are unsure about anything. Make sure your harness and helmet are fitted correctly and that you are comfortable with the equipment. Trust the guides and their expertise; they are there to ensure your safety and to help you have a great experience.

Zip-lining and canopy tours are suitable for a wide range of ages and fitness levels, but it is important to assess your own physical condition before embarking on the adventure. Some courses may have weight or age restrictions, so be sure to check with the tour operator in advance. If you have any medical conditions or concerns, consult with your doctor before participating in these activities.

CHAPTER 10

WELLNESS AND RELAXATION

Best Spas and Wellness Retreats

Fiji, with its stunning beaches, lush rainforests, and tranquil atmosphere, is an ideal destination for relaxation and rejuvenation. The islands are home to some of the world's best spas and wellness retreats, offering a wide range of treatments and experiences designed to refresh the mind, body, and spirit.

One of the most renowned wellness retreats in Fiji is the Likuliku Lagoon Resort, located on Malolo Island in the Mamanuca archipelago. This adults-only resort is known for its luxurious overwater bungalows, pristine beaches, and world-class spa facilities. The Tatadra Spa at Likuliku offers a serene environment where guests can indulge in a variety of treatments inspired by traditional Fijian healing practices. The spa menu includes massages, body wraps, facials, and exfoliation treatments, all using natural and locally sourced ingredients. The signature Fijian Bobo massage, a deep-tissue technique using coconut oil, is particularly popular and provides a deeply relaxing experience. The spa's tranquil setting, combined with the gentle sounds of the ocean, creates an idyllic atmosphere for relaxation and rejuvenation.

Another exceptional wellness retreat in Fiji is the Namale Resort and Spa, located on Vanua Levu near the town of Savusavu. Nestled amidst lush tropical gardens and overlooking the Koro Sea, Namale offers a luxurious and intimate retreat experience. The Namale Spa Sanctuary is an award-winning facility that provides a comprehensive range of treatments designed to promote wellness and relaxation. Guests can choose from massages, facials, hydrotherapy, and beauty treatments, all performed by skilled therapists using natural products. One of the highlights of the Namale Spa is the hydrotherapy room, which features a waterfall massage, aromatherapy pools, and a jacuzzi with stunning ocean views. The spa also offers yoga and meditation sessions, providing a holistic approach to wellness that nurtures both the body and mind.

For those seeking a more secluded and exclusive wellness experience, the Royal Davui Island Resort is an excellent choice. Located on a private island in the Beqa Lagoon, this adults-only resort offers a tranquil and intimate setting for relaxation and rejuvenation. The Davui Spa at Royal Davui provides a range of treatments inspired by traditional Fijian healing practices and modern wellness techniques. Guests can enjoy massages, facials, body scrubs, and wraps, all using natural ingredients such as coconut oil, tropical fruits, and marine extracts. The spa's open-air treatment rooms, with views of the lagoon and the sound of the waves, create a peaceful and calming environment. In addition to spa treatments, Royal Davui offers wellness activities such as yoga, snorkeling, and nature walks, allowing guests to connect with nature and enhance their overall well-being.

The Six Senses Fiji, located on Malolo Island, is another top wellness retreat known for its luxurious accommodations and holistic wellness programs. The Six Senses Spa offers a wide range of treatments designed to promote physical, mental, and emotional well-being. The spa menu includes massages, facials, body treatments, and wellness therapies such as acupuncture, Reiki, and Ayurveda. The signature Six Senses Integrated Wellness program provides personalized wellness plans based on a detailed analysis of the guest's health and lifestyle. This program includes a combination of treatments, nutrition, fitness, and mindfulness practices tailored to the individual's needs. The spa's serene setting, combined with the expertise of the therapists and wellness practitioners, ensures a comprehensive and transformative wellness experience.

On the island of Viti Levu, the InterContinental Fiji Golf Resort and Spa offers a luxurious wellness retreat with stunning views of Natadola Bay. The Spa InterContinental provides a range of treatments inspired by traditional Fijian rituals and modern wellness techniques. Guests can enjoy massages, facials, body treatments, and beauty services, all performed by skilled therapists using natural products. The spa's signature treatment, the Fijian Tropical Paradise Ritual, includes a coconut milk bath, a sugar cane body scrub, and a coconut oil massage, providing a deeply relaxing and rejuvenating experience. The spa also features a hydrotherapy area with a steam room, sauna, and Jacuzzi, allowing guests to unwind and detoxify in a tranquil environment.

Another notable wellness retreat in Fiji is the Jean-Michel Cousteau Resort, located on the island of Vanua Levu near Savusavu. This eco-friendly resort offers a holistic approach to wellness, combining luxurious accommodations, gourmet cuisine, and a range of wellness activities. The Bula Club Spa at Jean-Michel Cousteau Resort provides a variety of treatments designed to promote relaxation and well-being. Guests can enjoy massages, facials, body treatments, and beauty services, all using natural and organic products. The spa's open-air treatment rooms, surrounded by lush gardens and with views of the ocean, create a serene and peaceful environment. In addition to spa treatments, the resort offers yoga, meditation, and fitness classes, as well as activities such as snorkeling, diving, and nature walks, allowing guests to connect with nature and enhance their overall well-being.

For those seeking a wellness retreat that combines luxury with traditional Fijian culture, the Nanuku Auberge Resort is an excellent choice. Located on the Coral Coast of Viti Levu, this resort offers a range of wellness experiences designed to promote relaxation and rejuvenation. The Lomana Spa and Wellness Centre at Nanuku provides a variety of treatments inspired by traditional Fijian healing practices. Guests can enjoy massages, facials, body scrubs, and wraps, all using natural ingredients such as coconut oil, tropical fruits, and marine extracts. The spa also offers wellness programs that include yoga, meditation, fitness classes, and nutritional guidance, providing a holistic approach to well-being. The resort's beautiful beachfront setting, combined with the expertise of the therapists and wellness practitioners, ensures a transformative wellness experience.

Yoga and Meditation in Paradise

Practicing yoga and meditation in the idyllic surroundings of Fiji offers a unique and transformative experience, allowing individuals to deepen their practice while immersed in the natural beauty of this tropical paradise. Fiji's tranquil beaches, lush rainforests, and serene island atmosphere provide the perfect backdrop for relaxation, self-discovery, and inner peace.

Yoga, a practice that combines physical postures, breathing exercises, and meditation, is known for its numerous benefits to both physical and mental health. Regular practice can improve flexibility, strength, and balance, while also reducing stress and promoting a sense of calm and well-being. Meditation, often practiced alongside yoga, involves focusing the mind and eliminating distractions to achieve a state of heightened awareness and inner peace. Together, yoga and meditation can enhance overall health and well-being, making them ideal practices for anyone looking to rejuvenate and reconnect with themselves.

Fiji offers a variety of yoga and meditation retreats, each providing a unique environment and approach to these practices. One of the most renowned yoga retreats in Fiji is the Daku Resort, located on the island of Vanua Levu near Savusavu. Daku Resort offers a range of yoga retreats throughout the year, each led by experienced instructors who guide participants through daily yoga sessions, meditation practices, and workshops. The retreat's open-air yoga shala, overlooking the ocean and surrounded by lush gardens, provides a serene and inspiring setting for practice. Participants can also enjoy healthy, locally sourced meals, as well as optional activities such as snorkeling, diving, and nature walks, making it a holistic and enriching experience.

Another exceptional yoga and meditation retreat is the Fiji Beachouse, located on the Coral Coast of Viti Levu. This beachfront retreat offers daily yoga classes in a relaxed and welcoming environment, suitable for practitioners of all levels. The retreat's yoga pavilion, set amidst tropical gardens and with views of the ocean, provides a peaceful space for practice. In addition to yoga, the Fiji Beachouse offers guided meditation sessions, allowing participants to deepen their mindfulness practice and achieve a state of inner calm. The retreat also provides opportunities for guests to explore the local area, with activities such as kayaking, surfing, and cultural tours available.

For those seeking a more luxurious and secluded retreat experience, the Raiwasa Private Resort on Taveuni is an excellent choice. This exclusive retreat offers personalized yoga and meditation sessions tailored to the individual needs and preferences of each guest. The resort's stunning location, with panoramic views of the ocean and surrounding rainforest, provides a breathtaking backdrop for practice. Guests can enjoy private yoga classes on the beach, in the gardens, or on the resort's oceanfront deck, allowing for a truly immersive and tranquil experience. The Raiwasa Private Resort also offers wellness treatments, gourmet meals, and a range of outdoor activities, ensuring a comprehensive and rejuvenating retreat.

The Yoga and Wellness Retreat at the Jean-Michel Cousteau Resort on Vanua Levu is another notable option for those looking to combine yoga and meditation with luxury and eco-conscious living. This retreat offers daily yoga classes, meditation sessions, and wellness workshops, all led by experienced instructors. The resort's beautiful beachfront location and commitment to sustainability create a harmonious and inspiring environment for practice. Guests can also enjoy a range of wellness treatments at the resort's spa, as well as activities such as snorkeling, diving, and exploring the local marine environment.

Practicing yoga and meditation in Fiji provides a unique opportunity to connect with nature and find inner peace in a stunning and serene setting. The island's natural beauty, with its clear blue waters, white sandy beaches, and lush greenery, creates a perfect environment for relaxation and mindfulness. The sound of the waves, the warmth of the sun, and the gentle breeze all contribute to a sense of calm and well-being, enhancing the overall experience of yoga and meditation.

In addition to the structured retreats and classes, many resorts and wellness centers in Fiji offer drop-in yoga and meditation sessions, allowing visitors to incorporate these practices into their vacation at their own pace. These sessions are often held in beautiful outdoor locations, such as beachfront pavilions, garden gazebos, or open-air decks, providing a tranquil and inspiring setting for practice. Whether you are an experienced practitioner or a beginner, these sessions offer an accessible and enjoyable way to experience the benefits of yoga and meditation while enjoying the beauty of Fiji.

The benefits of practicing yoga and meditation in Fiji extend beyond the physical and mental health benefits. These practices also offer an opportunity for self-discovery and personal growth. The tranquil and nurturing environment of Fiji allows individuals to step away from the stresses and distractions of daily life, providing space for reflection and introspection. The practice of yoga and meditation encourages mindfulness, helping individuals to develop a deeper awareness of their thoughts, emotions, and physical sensations. This heightened awareness can lead to greater clarity, insight, and a sense of inner peace.

In addition to the structured yoga and meditation sessions, many retreats in Fiji also offer workshops and activities that complement these practices. These may include mindfulness and relaxation techniques, breathwork, journaling, and creative expression. These additional activities provide a holistic approach to wellness, supporting the mind, body, and spirit. They also offer opportunities for participants to explore new practices and develop skills that they can incorporate into their daily lives.

For those interested in exploring the cultural aspects of yoga and meditation, some retreats in Fiji also offer workshops and classes on traditional Fijian healing practices and spirituality. These may include sessions on traditional Fijian massage, herbal medicine, and ceremonies. These cultural experiences provide a deeper understanding of the local traditions and offer a unique perspective on wellness and healing.

When planning a yoga and meditation retreat in Fiji, it is important to consider a few practical tips to ensure a comfortable and enjoyable experience. First, choose a retreat or resort that aligns with your preferences and goals. Consider factors such as the location, the types of yoga and meditation offered, the instructors, and the overall atmosphere of the retreat. It is also important to check the schedule and availability of classes and workshops, as well as any additional activities or amenities offered.

Pack comfortable clothing suitable for yoga and meditation, as well as swimwear and casual attire for other activities. Bring a yoga mat if you prefer to use your own, although most retreats provide mats and other necessary equipment. It is also a good idea to bring a journal or notebook for reflection and note-taking during workshops and sessions.

Finally, approach the retreat with an open mind and a willingness to explore and grow. Yoga and meditation are practices that require patience and dedication, and each person's experience is unique. Allow yourself to fully immerse in the experience, embrace the beauty and tranquility of Fiji, and enjoy the journey of self-discovery and well-being.

Natural Hot Springs and Mud Baths

Fiji is known for its stunning natural beauty, and among its many attractions are the natural hot springs and mud baths, which offer a unique and rejuvenating experience for visitors. These natural wonders provide a perfect opportunity to relax, detoxify, and immerse yourself in the therapeutic benefits of geothermal activity.

One of the most well-known natural hot springs and mud baths in Fiji is located in the Sabeto Valley on the island of Viti Levu. The Sabeto Hot Springs and Mud Pool, often referred to as the "Sabeto Mud Baths," is a popular destination for both locals and tourists seeking relaxation and healing. The experience begins with a dip in the warm mud pool, where visitors cover themselves from head to toe in the rich, volcanic mud. The mud is believed to have detoxifying properties, drawing out impurities from the skin and leaving it feeling soft and smooth. After allowing the mud to dry and harden in the sun, visitors then rinse off in a series of hot spring pools, which are fed by geothermal waters rich in minerals.

The hot springs at Sabeto are naturally heated by the geothermal activity beneath the earth's surface. The warm waters are said to have therapeutic benefits, including improving circulation, relieving muscle and joint pain, and promoting relaxation. The combination of the mud bath and the hot springs creates a unique and invigorating experience that leaves visitors feeling refreshed and rejuvenated. The tranquil setting of the Sabeto Valley, surrounded by lush greenery and the sounds of nature, adds to the overall sense of peace and well-being.

Another popular destination for hot springs and mud baths in Fiji is the Tifajek Mud Pool and Hot Springs, also located in the Sabeto Valley. Similar to the Sabeto Mud Baths, the Tifajek Mud Pool offers a combination of mud baths and hot spring pools. Visitors begin by immersing themselves in the warm mud, which is rich in minerals and known for its skin-cleansing properties. After allowing the mud to dry, they then rinse off in a series of hot spring pools, enjoying the soothing and healing effects of the geothermal waters. The Tifajek Mud Pool is known for its friendly and welcoming atmosphere, with local guides providing information about the benefits of the mud and the hot springs, as well as the history and culture of the area.

The therapeutic benefits of hot springs and mud baths have been recognized for centuries, and Fiji's natural geothermal sites offer an ideal environment for these wellness treatments. The mineral-rich mud and warm waters are believed to have numerous health benefits, including detoxifying the skin, relieving stress, reducing inflammation, and improving circulation. The heat from the hot springs helps to relax muscles and joints, making it an effective treatment for conditions such as arthritis and muscle pain. The minerals found in the mud and hot springs, such as sulfur, magnesium, and potassium, are also beneficial for the skin, promoting a healthy and radiant complexion.

In addition to the physical benefits, the experience of visiting a hot spring or mud bath in Fiji also offers mental and emotional benefits. The act of immersing oneself in warm, soothing waters and allowing the body to relax can help to reduce stress and promote a sense of calm and well-being. The natural surroundings, with their lush greenery, fresh air, and tranquil atmosphere, further enhance the experience, providing a peaceful escape from the stresses of daily life. Many visitors find that the combination of the physical and mental relaxation leads to a deep sense of rejuvenation and revitalization.

While the Sabeto Valley is the most well-known area for hot springs and mud baths in Fiji, there are other geothermal sites scattered throughout the islands that offer similar experiences. On the island of Vanua Levu, near the town of Savusavu, there are several hot springs that provide a natural and therapeutic bathing experience. The hot springs in Savusavu are less developed than those in the Sabeto Valley, offering a more rustic and natural setting for visitors. The geothermal waters bubble up from beneath the earth's surface, creating warm pools that are perfect for soaking and relaxing. The mineral-rich waters are believed to have healing properties, making them a popular destination for those seeking natural wellness treatments.

The experience of visiting a hot spring or mud bath in Fiji is enhanced by the local culture and traditions that surround these natural sites. Many of the hot springs and mud baths are located in areas that are considered sacred by the local communities, and visitors are often welcomed with a traditional Fijian greeting and offered insights into the cultural significance of the site. The local guides and attendants are knowledgeable about the history and benefits of the geothermal waters and are happy to share their knowledge with visitors. This cultural aspect adds a deeper dimension to the experience, allowing visitors to connect with the local traditions and gain a greater appreciation for the natural wonders of Fiji.

When planning a visit to the hot springs and mud baths in Fiji, there are a few practical tips to keep in mind to ensure a comfortable and enjoyable experience. First, it is important to wear a swimsuit or clothing that you don't mind getting muddy, as the mud can stain fabrics. It is also a good idea to bring a towel and a change of clothes for after your visit. Many of the hot springs and mud baths provide basic facilities for rinsing off and changing, but bringing your own towel and toiletries can make the experience more comfortable.

Hydration is also important, as the heat from the hot springs can cause you to sweat and lose fluids. Be sure to drink plenty of water before and after your visit to stay hydrated. It is also a good idea to avoid alcohol and caffeine before visiting the hot springs, as these can dehydrate the body.

For those with sensitive skin or allergies, it is a good idea to test a small patch of skin with the mud or hot spring water before fully immersing yourself. While the mud and geothermal waters are generally safe and beneficial for most people, some individuals may have reactions to certain minerals or elements. If you have any concerns or medical conditions, it is always a good idea to consult with a healthcare professional before visiting a hot spring or mud bath.

Healthy Eating and Detox Programs

Healthy eating and detox programs in Fiji offer a unique opportunity to rejuvenate your body and mind while enjoying the natural beauty of the islands. Fiji's lush landscapes, fresh local produce, and tranquil environment create the perfect setting for a wellness retreat focused on nourishing your body with healthy food and cleansing your system through detox programs.

Healthy eating is essential for maintaining overall well-being and preventing chronic diseases. It involves consuming a balanced diet that includes a variety of nutrient-dense foods, such as fruits, vegetables, whole grains, lean proteins, and healthy fats. These foods provide the vitamins, minerals, and antioxidants necessary for optimal health. In addition to the nutritional benefits, healthy eating can improve energy levels, support mental clarity, and promote a healthy weight.

Detoxification, or detox, is the process of removing toxins from the body. Toxins can come from various sources, including processed foods, environmental pollutants, and stress. Detox programs typically involve a combination of dietary changes, hydration, and lifestyle practices aimed at supporting the body's natural detoxification processes. These programs often include the consumption of detoxifying foods and beverages, such as fruits, vegetables, herbal teas, and water, as well as practices like fasting, exercise, and relaxation techniques.

Fiji is home to several wellness retreats that offer comprehensive healthy eating and detox programs. One of the most renowned retreats is the Daku Resort, located on the island of Vanua Levu near Savusavu. Daku Resort offers a range of wellness retreats throughout the year, each focused on promoting health and well-being through nutritious food and detoxification. The retreat's culinary team prepares meals using fresh, locally sourced ingredients, ensuring that each dish is packed with nutrients and flavor. Guests can enjoy a variety of healthy meals, including vibrant salads, fresh seafood, tropical fruits, and homemade smoothies. In addition to healthy eating, the retreat offers detox programs that include juice fasting, herbal teas, and guided detoxification practices. These programs are designed to cleanse the body, boost energy levels, and support overall wellness.

Another exceptional wellness retreat in Fiji is the Namale Resort and Spa, located on Vanua Levu near Savusavu. Namale offers a luxurious and intimate retreat experience, with a strong emphasis on healthy eating and detoxification. The resort's chefs create gourmet meals using organic, locally sourced ingredients, ensuring that each dish is both nutritious and delicious. The menu includes a variety of plant-based dishes, fresh seafood, and tropical fruits, all prepared with a focus on health and wellness. In addition to healthy meals, Namale offers detox programs that include juice cleanses, herbal teas, and holistic treatments. Guests can also participate in wellness activities such as yoga, meditation, and fitness classes, providing a comprehensive approach to detoxification and well-being.

The Six Senses Fiji, located on Malolo Island, is another top wellness retreat known for its commitment to healthy living and detoxification. The Six Senses Spa offers a range of detox programs designed to cleanse the body and support overall health. These programs include juice fasting, detoxifying meals, and herbal teas, all prepared using fresh, organic ingredients. The spa also offers personalized wellness plans based on a detailed analysis of the guest's health and lifestyle. These plans include a combination of treatments, nutrition, fitness, and mindfulness practices tailored to the individual's needs. The Six Senses Fiji provides a holistic and transformative wellness experience, allowing guests to rejuvenate their bodies and minds in a serene and beautiful setting.

On the island of Viti Levu, the InterContinental Fiji Golf Resort and Spa offers a luxurious wellness retreat with a focus on healthy eating and detoxification. The resort's culinary team creates nutritious and delicious meals using fresh, locally sourced ingredients, with a menu that includes a variety of healthy options. Guests can enjoy dishes such as grilled fish, colorful salads, and tropical fruit platters, all prepared with a focus on health and wellness. The resort also offers detox programs that include juice cleanses, herbal teas, and holistic treatments. In addition to healthy eating and detoxification, guests can participate in wellness activities such as yoga, meditation, and fitness classes, providing a comprehensive approach to well-being.

The Raiwasa Private Resort on Taveuni is another excellent choice for those seeking a personalized and luxurious wellness retreat. This exclusive resort offers customized healthy eating and detox programs tailored to the individual needs and preferences of each guest. The resort's chefs prepare gourmet meals using fresh, organic ingredients, with a menu that includes a variety of plant-based dishes, fresh seafood, and tropical fruits. Guests can also participate in detox programs that include juice fasting, herbal teas, and holistic treatments. The resort's stunning location, with panoramic views of the ocean and surrounding rainforest, provides a breathtaking backdrop for relaxation and rejuvenation.

The benefits of participating in a healthy eating and detox program in Fiji extend beyond physical health. These programs also offer mental and emotional benefits, helping to reduce stress, improve mental clarity, and promote a sense of well-being. The act of nourishing the body with nutritious food and cleansing the system through detoxification can lead to a deeper connection with oneself and a greater appreciation for the body's natural ability to heal and rejuvenate. The tranquil and beautiful environment of Fiji enhances the overall experience, providing a peaceful escape from the stresses of daily life and allowing for true relaxation and rejuvenation.

In addition to the structured detox programs and healthy meals, many wellness retreats in Fiji offer workshops and activities that complement these practices. These may include cooking classes, nutritional counseling, mindfulness and relaxation techniques, and fitness classes. These additional activities provide a holistic approach to wellness, supporting the mind, body, and spirit. They also offer opportunities for participants to learn new skills and develop habits that they can incorporate into their daily lives.

For those interested in exploring the cultural aspects of healthy eating and detoxification, some retreats in Fiji also offer workshops and classes on traditional Fijian healing practices and cuisine. These may include sessions on traditional Fijian cooking, herbal medicine, and wellness rituals. These cultural experiences provide a deeper understanding of the local traditions and offer a unique perspective on wellness and healing.

When planning a healthy eating and detox retreat in Fiji, it is important to consider a few practical tips to ensure a comfortable and enjoyable experience. First, choose a retreat or resort that aligns with your preferences and goals. Consider factors such as the location, the types of detox programs offered, the culinary philosophy of the retreat, and the overall atmosphere. It is also important to check the schedule and availability of classes and workshops, as well as any additional activities or amenities offered.

Pack comfortable clothing suitable for yoga, meditation, and other wellness activities, as well as swimwear and casual attire for other activities. Bring any personal items you may need, such as toiletries, a journal for reflection and note-taking, and any medications or supplements you may require. It is also a good idea to bring a reusable water bottle to stay hydrated throughout your stay.

Finally, approach the retreat with an open mind and a willingness to explore and grow. Healthy eating and detox programs require dedication and commitment, and each person's experience is unique. Allow yourself to fully immerse in the experience, embrace the beauty and tranquility of Fiji, and enjoy the journey of self-discovery and well-being.

CHAPTER 11

SHOPPING AND SOUVENIRS

Markets and Bazaars to Explore

Exploring markets and bazaars in Fiji offers a vibrant and immersive experience that allows visitors to connect with the local culture, sample traditional foods, and find unique handmade crafts. These bustling markets are the heart of Fijian communities, where vendors gather to sell fresh produce, artisanal goods, and traditional handicrafts.

One of the most prominent markets in Fiji is the Suva Municipal Market, located in the capital city of Suva on the island of Viti Levu. This market is one of the largest and most diverse in the country, offering a wide range of fresh produce, seafood, spices, and traditional Fijian foods. As you walk through the market, you'll be greeted by the vibrant colors of tropical fruits and vegetables, the enticing aromas of local dishes, and the friendly smiles of the vendors. The market is a great place to sample Fijian staples such as cassava, taro, and fresh fish, as well as exotic fruits like papaya, pineapple, and passionfruit. The Suva Municipal Market also features a section dedicated to handicrafts, where you can find woven baskets, mats, and traditional Fijian pottery. This market provides a lively and authentic glimpse into the daily life of Fijians and is a must-visit for anyone wanting to experience the local culture.

Another significant market is the Nadi Market, located in the town of Nadi on Viti Levu. Nadi Market is known for its fresh produce, with vendors selling a variety of fruits, vegetables, and herbs. The market is particularly famous for its kava, a traditional Fijian drink made from the root of the kava plant. Kava has cultural and social significance in Fiji and is often consumed during ceremonies and gatherings. At Nadi Market, you can purchase kava root and learn about its preparation and cultural importance from the vendors. In addition to fresh produce, the market also features stalls selling handmade crafts, jewelry, and souvenirs. The bustling atmosphere and friendly

Unique Fijian Souvenirs to Bring Home

Fiji is a country rich in culture and natural beauty, offering a wide range of unique souvenirs that capture the essence of the islands. Bringing home a piece of Fiji allows you to remember your trip and share its magic with others. The souvenirs found in Fiji are often handmade and reflect the traditional crafts and artistry of the Fijian people.

One of the most iconic Fijian souvenirs is the tapa cloth, also known as masi. Tapa cloth is made from the bark of the paper mulberry tree and is traditionally used in various Fijian ceremonies and rituals. The bark is beaten into thin sheets and then decorated with intricate patterns and designs using natural dyes. These designs often include motifs that represent Fijian culture and heritage, such as geometric shapes, animals, and plants. Tapa cloth can be used as wall hangings, table runners, or even framed as artwork. Purchasing a piece of tapa cloth not only brings home a beautiful and unique souvenir but also supports local artisans who keep this traditional craft alive.

Another unique Fijian souvenir is the kava bowl, used in the traditional preparation and serving of kava, a drink made from the root of the kava plant. Kava has significant cultural and social importance in Fiji, often consumed during ceremonies and social gatherings. The kava bowl, or tanoa, is usually made from wood and features a distinctive rounded shape with short legs. The bowl is often carved with intricate designs, making it both a functional item and a piece of art. Bringing home a kava bowl is a wonderful way to remember the cultural experiences you had in Fiji and to share the tradition of kava with friends and family.

Handcrafted wooden items are also popular souvenirs in Fiji. The islands are home to skilled woodcarvers who create a variety of items, from small trinkets to large sculptures. Wooden masks, bowls, and utensils are commonly found at local markets and craft shops. Each piece is typically carved by hand and may feature traditional Fijian motifs and designs. Wooden items make excellent souvenirs because they are both beautiful and practical, and they showcase the craftsmanship of Fijian artisans.

Fijian jewelry is another excellent choice for a unique souvenir. Traditional Fijian jewelry often incorporates natural materials such as shells, coconut shells, and seeds. Necklaces, bracelets, and earrings made from these materials are not only beautiful but also reflect the natural beauty of the islands. One popular type of jewelry is made from black pearls, which are farmed in the waters around Fiji. Black pearls are known for their unique luster and color, making them a special and luxurious souvenir. Additionally, many artisans create jewelry using traditional techniques, such as weaving and beadwork, resulting in pieces that are both unique and culturally significant.

For those interested in Fijian textiles, a woven mat or basket is a perfect souvenir. Weaving is a traditional craft in Fiji, with women typically making mats and baskets from pandanus leaves or coconut fronds. These items are often used in everyday life in Fiji, as well as in ceremonial contexts. The mats and baskets are not only functional but also beautifully crafted, with intricate patterns and designs. Bringing home a woven mat or basket is a way to appreciate the skill and artistry of Fijian weavers and to incorporate a piece of Fijian culture into your home.

Fijian pottery is another unique souvenir that reflects the rich cultural heritage of the islands. Traditional Fijian pottery is often made using methods passed down through generations, with artisans shaping the clay by hand and firing it in open pits. The pottery is typically decorated with simple, yet elegant designs that reflect the natural beauty of Fiji.

Common items include bowls, vases, and figurines, each piece unique and handcrafted. Purchasing Fijian pottery supports local artisans and provides a beautiful and functional souvenir that can be used and displayed in your home.

For those who appreciate natural beauty and skincare, Fijian coconut oil is a must-have souvenir. Coconut oil has been used in Fiji for centuries for its moisturizing and healing properties. It is made by extracting the oil from the meat of mature coconuts, resulting in a pure and natural product. Fijian coconut oil is often used in skincare and haircare products, providing a natural way to nourish and protect the skin and hair. Many local producers offer coconut oil that is sustainably sourced and handcrafted, ensuring a high-quality product. Bringing home Fijian coconut oil allows you to experience the benefits of this natural remedy and to support sustainable practices in Fiji.

Another delightful souvenir is Fijian honey. Fiji is home to diverse flora, and the bees produce honey that is rich in flavor and nutrients. Fijian honey is often harvested using traditional methods and is available in various forms, including raw, liquid, and creamed. The unique flavor of Fijian honey makes it a delicious and healthy souvenir that can be enjoyed long after your trip. Additionally, purchasing local honey supports sustainable beekeeping practices and helps to preserve the natural environment of Fiji.

For those who enjoy culinary delights, Fijian spices and teas are excellent souvenirs. Fiji's tropical climate is ideal for growing a variety of spices, including ginger, turmeric, and vanilla. These spices are often available at local markets and make for flavorful and aromatic souvenirs. Additionally, Fijian tea, particularly the herbal teas made from local plants and herbs, is a wonderful way to bring home the flavors of Fiji. These teas are often handcrafted and packaged beautifully, making them perfect gifts for friends and family.

Lastly, a unique and meaningful souvenir from Fiji is a traditional Fijian musical instrument. Instruments such as the lali (a wooden slit drum) or the derua (bamboo percussion instrument) are used in traditional Fijian music and dance. These instruments are often handcrafted and decorated with intricate designs. Bringing home a Fijian musical instrument not only provides a unique souvenir but also allows you to share the sounds and rhythms of Fiji with others.

CHAPTER 12

DINING AND NIGHTLIFE

Top Restaurants for Fine Dining

Fiji is not only a paradise of stunning beaches and vibrant culture but also a destination that offers a diverse and exquisite culinary scene. For travelers seeking a fine dining experience, Fiji provides a range of top-tier restaurants that blend local flavors with international cuisine, offering dishes that are as visually stunning as they are delicious.

One of the premier destinations for fine dining in Fiji is the renowned "Wicked Walu" restaurant, located on the private island of Yanuca at the Shangri-La's Fijian Resort & Spa. This restaurant offers a picturesque setting, perched over the lagoon with stunning ocean views. The menu at Wicked Walu focuses on fresh seafood, with dishes like grilled lobster, crab cakes, and a variety of fish cooked to perfection. The chefs here emphasize the use of locally sourced ingredients, ensuring that each dish is infused with the flavors of Fiji. The elegant ambiance, combined with the attentive service, makes dining at Wicked Walu a truly memorable experience.

Another top-notch dining establishment is "Flying Fish," situated at the Sheraton Fiji Resort on Denarau Island. Flying Fish is known for its innovative approach to seafood and its commitment to sustainability. The restaurant's open-air design provides a breezy, tropical atmosphere, making it the perfect place to enjoy dishes such as yellowfin tuna, coral trout, and the restaurant's signature coconut prawn curry. The chefs at Flying Fish are dedicated to showcasing the best of Fijian and Pacific Rim cuisine, creating a menu that is both creative and authentic.

For those seeking a blend of tradition and luxury, "Navutu Stars Resort Restaurant" on Yaqeta Island in the Yasawas offers an exceptional dining experience. This restaurant combines Fijian culinary traditions with Mediterranean influences, resulting in a unique fusion cuisine. The menu features dishes like Fijian kokoda (a local version of ceviche), freshly caught fish, and a variety of pasta and meat dishes. The use of organic produce from the resort's own garden adds an extra layer of freshness to each meal. Dining at Navutu Stars is an intimate experience, with only a few tables available, ensuring personalized service and a serene atmosphere.

In the heart of Nadi, "The Grace Road Kitchen" stands out as a fine dining gem. This restaurant is part of the Grace Road Group, known for its dedication to sustainable farming and high-quality produce. The menu at Grace Road Kitchen is diverse, offering everything from fresh salads and grilled meats to traditional Korean dishes. The chefs here take pride in using ingredients from the Grace Road Farm, ensuring that each dish is not only delicious but also healthy and sustainable. The modern, elegant setting of the restaurant provides a perfect backdrop for a refined dining experience.

On the island of Taveuni, "The Terraces Restaurant" at Taveuni Palms Resort offers an exclusive and luxurious dining experience. The Terraces is known for its breathtaking views of the ocean and its commitment to personalized service. The menu is a celebration of local flavors, with dishes such as grilled mahi-mahi, seared scallops, and Fijian-style lamb. The use of locally sourced, organic ingredients ensures that each dish is fresh and flavorful. Dining at The Terraces is an intimate affair, with private dining options available for those looking to celebrate a special occasion.

"The Beach House" at Turtle Island Resort is another must-visit for fine dining enthusiasts. This restaurant offers a unique farm-to-table dining experience, with a menu that changes daily based on the freshest available ingredients. Guests can enjoy dishes such as coconut-crusted prawns, Fijian-style chicken curry, and a variety of vegetarian options. The Beach House emphasizes the use of organic produce from the resort's own gardens, as well as fresh seafood caught daily. The stunning beachfront location and the personalized service make dining at The Beach House a truly unforgettable experience.

For a modern twist on traditional Fijian cuisine, "Ports O' Call" at the Sheraton Fiji Resort is a top choice. This restaurant is designed to resemble a classic ocean liner, providing a unique and sophisticated dining atmosphere. The menu features a range of gourmet dishes, including prime cuts of meat, fresh seafood, and decadent desserts. The chefs at Ports O' Call are known for their attention to detail and their ability to create dishes that are both visually stunning and delicious. The impeccable service and the elegant setting make this restaurant a standout choice for fine dining in Fiji.

On the island of Viti Levu, "Vuda Marina Restaurant" offers a delightful dining experience with a focus on fresh, local ingredients. The menu features a variety of dishes, including seafood platters, grilled steaks, and vegetarian options. The restaurant's open-air design provides beautiful views of the marina and the surrounding landscape, creating a relaxing and enjoyable dining environment. The chefs at Vuda Marina are committed to using sustainable ingredients and supporting local farmers and fishermen, ensuring that each dish is both delicious and environmentally friendly.

For those visiting Suva, "Tiko's Floating Restaurant" offers a unique dining experience on a converted ship moored in Suva Harbor. This restaurant is known for its seafood dishes, with a menu that includes fresh lobster, grilled fish, and prawn cocktails. The nautical-themed décor and the gentle sway of the ship create a memorable dining atmosphere. Tiko's Floating Restaurant also offers a range of international dishes, ensuring that there is something for everyone. The friendly service and the unique setting make this restaurant a popular choice for both locals and tourists.

Lastly, "The Wicked Walu" at the Shangri-La's Fijian Resort & Spa is a must-visit for those seeking a fine dining experience with a focus on seafood. The restaurant is located on its own private island, accessible by a short causeway, and offers stunning views of the surrounding lagoon. The menu features a variety of fresh seafood dishes, including grilled lobster, seafood platters, and Fijian-style fish curry. The elegant setting, combined with the impeccable service, makes dining at The Wicked Walu a truly unforgettable experience.

Best Local Eateries for Authentic Fijian Food

Experiencing authentic Fijian food is a must for any visitor to Fiji. The local cuisine is a rich blend of fresh seafood, tropical fruits, root vegetables, and traditional cooking methods that reflect the island's cultural heritage.

One of the top spots to savor traditional Fijian food is Tu's Place in Nadi. This local favorite is well-loved for its hearty portions and friendly atmosphere. The menu features a variety of authentic Fijian dishes, including kokoda, which is marinated raw fish in coconut milk, a dish similar to ceviche. Another popular item is lovo, a traditional Fijian feast cooked in an underground oven, which includes meats, fish, and root vegetables wrapped in banana leaves and slow-cooked to perfection. Tu's Place is also known for its fresh seafood and tropical fruit salads, making it a great place to experience the true flavors of Fiji.

In the heart of Suva, Eden Bistro & Bar offers a delightful experience of local cuisine with a modern twist. The restaurant prides itself on using fresh, local ingredients to create dishes that are both authentic and innovative. One of the standout dishes is palusami, which consists of taro leaves filled with coconut cream and onions, wrapped and cooked until tender. Eden Bistro also offers a variety of seafood dishes, including grilled fish and octopus, showcasing the rich marine resources of Fiji. The ambiance of Eden Bistro, with its cozy setting and attentive service, makes it a perfect spot to enjoy Fijian hospitality and cuisine.

For a more rustic and traditional dining experience, Tiko's Floating Restaurant in Suva provides a unique setting on a converted ship moored in the harbor. This restaurant is renowned for its seafood, which is a staple of Fijian cuisine. You can enjoy dishes like fish in miti sauce, which is a coconut milk-based sauce with onions and chilies, enhancing the natural flavors of the fish. The restaurant also serves rourou, a dish made from the leaves of the taro plant, cooked in coconut milk and often served with fish or meat. The nautical ambiance of Tiko's Floating Restaurant adds to the charm of dining here, making it a memorable experience.

In Lautoka, The Fiji Orchid is another excellent place to sample authentic Fijian food. This restaurant, located within a beautiful garden setting, offers a menu that emphasizes traditional Fijian dishes prepared with fresh, local ingredients. One of the highlights is the traditional Fijian curry, made with local spices, vegetables, and either chicken, fish, or lamb. The use of coconut milk and fresh herbs gives the curry a distinctive Fijian flavor. The Fiji Orchid also serves vakalolo, a traditional dessert made from cassava, coconut cream, and sugar, steamed in banana leaves. The serene setting and the delicious food make The Fiji Orchid a must-visit for anyone interested in Fijian cuisine.

For a more casual dining experience, Bulaccino Café in Nadi offers a range of local dishes in a relaxed, café-style setting. The café sources many of its ingredients from its own organic farm, ensuring freshness and quality. Popular dishes include kokoda, fish and chips made with local fish, and fresh salads featuring tropical fruits and vegetables. Bulaccino Café also offers a selection of baked goods, including traditional Fijian coconut buns and cakes. The combination of good food, friendly service, and a laid-back atmosphere makes Bulaccino Café a favorite among both locals and tourists.

In the small town of Sigatoka, Sigatoka River Safari not only offers a thrilling river adventure but also a chance to experience authentic Fijian food. The safari includes a visit to a local village where you can participate in a traditional lovo feast. The lovo is prepared by the villagers and includes a variety of meats, fish, and root vegetables cooked in an underground oven. The flavors are rich and smoky, offering a true taste of traditional Fijian cooking. This experience is enhanced by the warm hospitality of the villagers, making it a highlight of any visit to Sigatoka.

Another great spot to try authentic Fijian food is Baka Blues Café in Pacific Harbour. This café offers a laid-back atmosphere with live music and a menu that features both Fijian and international dishes. One of the standout items is the kokoda, served with fresh vegetables and a side of dalo, which is boiled taro root. The café also offers a range of grilled seafood and meats, all cooked with local spices and ingredients. The friendly staff and the vibrant atmosphere make Baka Blues Café a great place to relax and enjoy some delicious Fijian food.

For those visiting the island of Taveuni, Makaira Resort offers a fantastic dining experience that highlights local ingredients and traditional cooking methods. The resort's restaurant, known as the "Top of the Tropic," features a menu that changes daily based on the freshest available ingredients. Guests can enjoy dishes like grilled walu, a type of local fish, served with a coconut and lime sauce, or a traditional Fijian fish stew made with coconut milk and root vegetables. The use of fresh herbs and spices from the resort's garden adds depth and flavor to each dish, making dining at Makaira Resort a truly special experience.

Nightlife: Bars, Clubs, and Entertainment

Fiji is not only known for its stunning beaches and vibrant culture but also for its lively nightlife that offers a range of experiences for visitors. From bustling bars and energetic clubs to cultural entertainment and live music, the nightlife in Fiji is as diverse as it is exciting.

One of the key spots for nightlife in Fiji is Nadi, a bustling town that serves as a gateway to the islands. Nadi has a variety of bars and clubs that cater to different tastes. A popular spot is Ed's Bar, known for its laid-back atmosphere and great music. This bar is a favorite among locals and tourists alike, offering a mix of live music and DJ sets. The outdoor seating area is perfect for enjoying a drink while soaking in the tropical vibes. Ed's Bar also hosts themed nights and special events, making it a lively place to spend an evening.

Another notable venue in Nadi is Ice Bar, which is famous for its vibrant atmosphere and stylish décor. This bar is a hotspot for both locals and visitors, featuring a spacious dance floor and an impressive selection of cocktails. The music ranges from local Fijian tunes to international hits, ensuring a fun night out. Ice Bar is also known for its friendly staff and excellent service, making it a must-visit for anyone looking to experience the nightlife in Nadi.

For those who enjoy a more relaxed and intimate setting, Sitar Restaurant and Bar in Nadi offers a unique blend of

Indian cuisine and a cozy bar atmosphere. The bar area is perfect for enjoying a quiet drink with friends, with a selection of local beers, wines, and cocktails. The restaurant also features live music on certain nights, adding to the overall experience. Sitar Restaurant and Bar is an excellent choice for those looking to enjoy a delicious meal followed by a relaxed evening with drinks and music.

Moving to the capital city of Suva, the nightlife scene becomes even more diverse and vibrant. O'Reilly's Bar is one of the most popular nightlife spots in Suva, known for its lively atmosphere and wide range of drinks. The bar features a spacious outdoor area, perfect for enjoying the warm Fijian nights. O'Reilly's Bar hosts regular events, including live music, DJ nights, and themed parties, ensuring there is always something happening. The friendly crowd and energetic vibe make it a great place to socialize and have fun.

Another standout venue in Suva is The Bad Dog Café, which offers a unique blend of bar, café, and live music venue. This place is perfect for those who enjoy a more eclectic nightlife experience, with a menu that includes both local and international dishes. The bar area serves a variety of cocktails, beers, and wines, while the stage hosts live music performances from local and international artists. The Bad Dog Café is known for its relaxed and welcoming atmosphere, making it a favorite among locals and expats.

For a more upscale experience, Traps Bar in Suva offers a sophisticated setting with a stylish interior and an extensive drink menu. Traps Bar is a popular spot for both after-work drinks and late-night partying, featuring a mix of lounge areas and a lively dance floor. The bar is known for its expertly crafted cocktails and top-notch service, making it a great choice for those looking to enjoy a classy night out. Traps Bar also hosts special events and themed nights, adding to the overall excitement.

On Denarau Island, a popular tourist destination near Nadi, the nightlife is centered around the luxurious resorts and their offerings. Cardo's Steakhouse & Cocktail Bar is a notable venue that combines great food with a vibrant bar scene. Located in the Port Denarau Marina, Cardo's offers stunning views of the marina and a lively atmosphere. The bar serves a wide range of cocktails, beers, and wines, and the outdoor seating area is perfect for enjoying the tropical evenings. Cardo's also features live music and entertainment, making it a great place to relax and unwind.

For those staying on Denarau Island, the Hard Rock Café offers a fun and energetic nightlife experience. Known for its rock-and-roll theme and lively atmosphere, the Hard Rock Café features a spacious bar area, a dance floor, and regular live music performances. The drink menu includes classic cocktails, local beers, and a selection of wines. The Hard Rock Café is a great place to enjoy a fun night out with friends, dancing to live music and enjoying the vibrant ambiance.

In the Mamanuca Islands, the nightlife is centered around the resort bars and beach clubs. Cloud 9 is one of the most unique and popular spots, offering a floating bar experience in the middle of the ocean. This two-level platform features a bar, wood-fired pizza oven, and sun loungers, providing a perfect setting for a day of relaxation and fun. As the sun sets, Cloud 9 transforms into a lively venue with music, dancing, and stunning views of the ocean. The combination of a unique setting and a vibrant atmosphere makes Cloud 9 a must-visit for anyone in the Mamanuca Islands.

For a more traditional Fijian experience, Robinson Crusoe Island offers a cultural night that includes traditional Fijian dance performances, fire shows, and a traditional lovo feast. The island's cultural night provides a unique opportunity to experience Fijian culture and hospitality, with the evening culminating in a lively celebration under the stars. This experience is perfect for those looking to enjoy a more authentic and cultural aspect of Fijian nightlife.

For visitors to the Coral Coast, The Beach Bar & Grill at the Outrigger Fiji Beach Resort offers a lively and relaxed nightlife experience. This beachfront bar features a casual atmosphere with live music, fire dances, and a great selection of drinks. The Beach Bar & Grill is known for its friendly service and beautiful ocean views, making it a perfect spot to enjoy a laid-back evening by the beach.

Food Festivals and Culinary Events

Fiji is not only a paradise for beach lovers and adventure seekers but also a haven for food enthusiasts. The country's rich culinary heritage is celebrated through various food festivals and culinary events that offer visitors a taste of Fijian culture and cuisine. These events showcase the diverse flavors of Fiji, from traditional Fijian dishes to international culinary delights, and provide an excellent opportunity for food lovers to indulge in unique gastronomic experiences.

One of the most prominent culinary events in Fiji is the Bula Festival, held annually in Nadi. This week-long festival is a vibrant celebration of Fijian culture, featuring a wide array of activities, including music, dance, and food. The Bula Festival's food stalls offer a variety of traditional Fijian dishes, such as lovo (meat and vegetables cooked in an underground oven), kokoda (marinated raw fish in coconut milk), and rourou (taro leaves cooked in coconut milk). Visitors can also sample other Pacific Island and international cuisines, making it a diverse culinary experience. The festival's lively atmosphere, combined with the delicious food, makes it a must-visit event for any food enthusiast.

Another significant event is the Hibiscus Festival, held in Suva, the capital city of Fiji. The Hibiscus Festival is one of the oldest and most celebrated festivals in Fiji, attracting thousands of visitors each year. This week-long event features a wide range of activities, including a beauty pageant, cultural performances, and a bustling food fair. The food fair is a highlight of the festival, offering an extensive selection of Fijian and international dishes. Visitors can enjoy traditional Fijian foods like palusami (taro leaves filled with coconut cream), fresh seafood, and tropical fruits, as well as Indian, Chinese, and other international cuisines. The Hibiscus Festival provides an excellent opportunity to explore the diverse culinary landscape of Fiji while enjoying the vibrant cultural festivities.

The Sugar Festival, held in Lautoka, is another notable food festival in Fiji. Lautoka, known as the "Sugar City," is the center of Fiji's sugar industry, and the Sugar Festival celebrates this vital aspect of the country's economy. The festival features a variety of activities, including parades, music, dance, and food stalls. The food stalls offer a range of dishes that highlight the use of sugar and other local ingredients, such as sweet pastries, cakes, and desserts. Visitors can also enjoy savory dishes like curries, barbecued meats, and fresh seafood. The Sugar Festival is a great way to experience the local cuisine and learn about the importance of the sugar industry in Fiji.

For seafood lovers, the Lami Seafood Festival is a must-visit event. Held in the town of Lami, near Suva, this festival celebrates Fiji's rich marine resources and the local fishing industry. The Lami Seafood Festival features a wide array of seafood dishes, including grilled fish, prawns, crabs, and lobsters, as well as traditional Fijian seafood dishes like kokoda and ika vakalolo (fish cooked in coconut milk). The festival also includes cooking demonstrations, where visitors can learn how to prepare various seafood dishes using traditional Fijian methods. The Lami Seafood Festival provides a fantastic opportunity to indulge in fresh and delicious seafood while enjoying the beautiful coastal scenery.

The Fiji Street Food Festival, held in various locations across the country, is another event that food enthusiasts should not miss. This festival celebrates the vibrant street food culture in Fiji, offering a wide variety of dishes that reflect the country's diverse culinary heritage. Visitors can sample Fijian street food favorites like roti (Indian flatbread filled with curry), barbecue pork buns, and fried cassava chips, as well as international street foods like kebabs, dumplings, and tacos. The Fiji Street Food Festival also features live music and entertainment, creating a lively and enjoyable atmosphere. This festival is an excellent way to experience the flavors of Fiji's street food scene and discover new and exciting dishes.

For those interested in sustainable and organic farming, the Sigatoka Farmers Carnival is a notable event. Held in the town of Sigatoka, known as the "Salad Bowl of Fiji," this carnival celebrates the local farming community and their produce. The event features a variety of activities, including parades, music, dance, and food stalls offering fresh and organic produce. Visitors can enjoy dishes made from locally grown fruits and vegetables, as well as traditional Fijian foods like lovo and palusami. The Sigatoka Farmers Carnival also includes cooking demonstrations and workshops on sustainable farming practices, providing an educational and delicious experience.

The Thurston Food and Wine Festival, held in Suva, is a more upscale culinary event that showcases the best of Fijian and international cuisine. This festival features a wide range of food and wine stalls, offering gourmet dishes prepared by some of the best chefs in Fiji. Visitors can enjoy a variety of foods, from fresh seafood and grilled meats to artisanal cheeses and gourmet desserts. The festival also includes wine tastings, where visitors can sample a selection of fine wines from Fiji and around the world. The Thurston Food and Wine Festival provides a sophisticated and enjoyable culinary experience, perfect for food and wine connoisseurs.

Another notable event is the Fiji National Agriculture Show, which highlights the country's agricultural sector and its contribution to the local cuisine. Held in various locations across Fiji, this show features a variety of activities, including agricultural exhibits, livestock displays, and food stalls. Visitors can sample a range of dishes made from locally grown produce, including fresh fruits, vegetables, and meats. The show also includes cooking demonstrations and workshops on sustainable farming practices, providing an educational and enjoyable experience. The Fiji National Agriculture Show is an excellent opportunity to learn about the country's agricultural industry and its impact on the local cuisine.

For those interested in Indian cuisine, the Diwali Festival in Fiji offers a fantastic culinary experience. Diwali, the Hindu festival of lights, is widely celebrated in Fiji, which has a significant Indian population. During the festival, families prepare a variety of traditional Indian sweets and savory dishes, such as gulab jamun (milk-based sweets), samosas (fried pastries filled with spiced potatoes), and biryani (spiced rice with meat or vegetables). Many communities also host Diwali fairs, where visitors can sample these delicious foods and enjoy cultural performances. The Diwali Festival provides a unique opportunity to experience the rich flavors of Indian cuisine and celebrate one of Fiji's major cultural festivals.

Lastly, the Fijian Cultural and Food Festival, held in various locations across the country, is a celebration of Fijian culture and cuisine. This festival features a wide range of activities, including traditional dance performances, music, arts and crafts, and food stalls. Visitors can enjoy a variety of traditional Fijian dishes, such as lovo, kokoda, and palusami, as well as other Pacific Island and international cuisines. The festival also includes cooking demonstrations and workshops on Fijian culinary traditions, providing an educational and enjoyable experience. The Fijian Cultural and Food Festival is a great way to immerse yourself in the country's rich cultural heritage and enjoy its delicious cuisine.

CHAPTER 13

PRACTICAL INFORMATION FOR TRAVELERS

Currency and Banking

Fiji, known for its stunning islands and rich cultural heritage, also has a well-structured currency and banking system that caters to both locals and visitors. Understanding the currency and banking practices in Fiji can significantly enhance your travel experience, ensuring that you can manage your finances efficiently and avoid any potential inconveniences.

The official currency of Fiji is the Fijian dollar, abbreviated as FJD and often symbolized as $. The Fijian dollar is subdivided into 100 cents. The Reserve Bank of Fiji issues the currency, which comes in both coins and banknotes. Coins are available in denominations of 5, 10, 20, and 50 cents, as well as 1 and 2 dollars. Banknotes are issued in denominations of 5, 10, 20, 50, and 100 dollars. Each banknote features significant historical and cultural imagery, reflecting the rich heritage of Fiji.

When traveling to Fiji, it is essential to have some Fijian dollars on hand for small purchases, as not all vendors, especially in remote areas, accept credit or debit cards. You can exchange your home currency for Fijian dollars at banks, exchange bureaus, and some hotels. It is advisable to compare exchange rates and fees at different places to get the best deal. Banks typically offer better exchange rates compared to hotels and exchange bureaus. Major international airports, including Nadi International Airport and Suva's Nausori Airport, also have currency exchange counters where you can obtain Fijian dollars upon arrival.

Fiji's banking system is well-developed, with several commercial banks operating across the country. The major banks in Fiji include:

1. **ANZ (Australia and New Zealand Banking Group):** ANZ is one of the largest banks in Fiji, offering a wide range of banking services, including personal and business banking, loans, mortgages, and investment services. ANZ has a comprehensive network of branches and ATMs across Fiji, ensuring easy access to banking services.

2. **Westpac:** Another major bank in Fiji, Westpac provides various financial services, including savings and checking accounts, personal and business loans, and credit cards. Westpac also has an extensive network of branches and ATMs, making it convenient for both locals and tourists to access their services.

3. **Bank of South Pacific (BSP):** BSP is a prominent bank in the South Pacific region, including Fiji. It offers a range of banking products and services, such as personal and business accounts, loans, and foreign exchange services.

BSP has numerous branches and ATMs throughout Fiji, ensuring widespread access to banking facilities.

4. HFC Bank: Home Finance Company Limited, or HFC Bank, is a locally owned bank in Fiji. It provides various banking services, including personal and business accounts, loans, and investment services. HFC Bank has several branches and ATMs, mainly in urban areas.

5. Baroda: Bank of Baroda is an international bank with a presence in Fiji. It offers a range of banking services, including personal and business banking, loans, and foreign exchange services. The bank has branches and ATMs in major cities and towns in Fiji.

ATMs are widely available in urban areas and tourist destinations in Fiji, making it easy to withdraw cash as needed. Most ATMs accept international debit and credit cards, including Visa, MasterCard, and American Express. However, it is essential to check with your home bank about any fees associated with international ATM withdrawals. It is also advisable to inform your bank of your travel plans to avoid any issues with card usage while abroad.

Credit and debit cards are widely accepted in hotels, restaurants, and larger stores in urban areas and tourist destinations. However, smaller vendors, markets, and businesses in remote areas may only accept cash. Therefore, it is a good idea to carry some cash for small purchases and in case you encounter places that do not accept cards.

Traveler's checks are another option for carrying money while traveling in Fiji. They are safer than carrying large amounts of cash and can be replaced if lost or stolen. Traveler's checks can be exchanged for Fijian dollars at banks and some hotels. However, their usage has declined with the advent of ATMs and credit cards, so it is advisable to check their acceptability before relying on them entirely.

Mobile banking is becoming increasingly popular in Fiji, with many banks offering mobile banking apps and services. These apps allow you to manage your accounts, transfer money, pay bills, and perform other banking transactions from your smartphone. Mobile banking provides a convenient and secure way to manage your finances while traveling.

When handling money in Fiji, it is essential to be aware of the security measures to protect your finances. Here are some practical tips:

1. Keep Your Money Safe: Use a money belt or a secure wallet to keep your cash, cards, and important documents safe. Avoid carrying large amounts of cash, and use hotel safes to store your valuables.

2. Be Cautious at ATMs: When using ATMs, choose machines located in well-lit and secure areas, such as bank branches or shopping centers. Be aware of your surroundings and shield your PIN when entering it. If you encounter any issues with the ATM, contact your bank immediately.

3. Monitor Your Accounts: Regularly check your bank and credit card statements to ensure there are no unauthorized transactions. Report any suspicious activity to your bank promptly.

4. Use Secure Payment Methods: When paying with credit or debit cards, ensure the transaction is processed in front of you. Avoid letting your card out of sight, especially in unfamiliar places.

5. Inform Your Bank: Notify your bank of your travel plans to avoid any issues with card usage while abroad. This can prevent your card from being flagged for suspicious activity.

6. Exchange Money Wisely: Compare exchange rates and fees at different places to get the best deal when exchanging currency. Banks typically offer better exchange rates compared to hotels and exchange bureaus.

7. Be Aware of Scams: Be cautious of anyone offering unsolicited assistance with financial transactions or money exchange. Use reputable banks and exchange bureaus for all currency transactions.

Understanding the currency and banking system in Fiji is essential for managing your finances efficiently during your stay. The Fijian dollar is the official currency, and it is advisable to have some cash on hand for small purchases and places that do not accept cards. Fiji's banking system is well-developed, with several commercial banks offering a range of services. ATMs are widely available, and credit and debit cards are accepted in most urban areas and tourist destinations. By following practical tips for handling money and being aware of security measures, you can ensure a smooth and enjoyable financial experience while exploring the beautiful islands of Fiji.

Communication and Internet Access

Communication and internet access are essential aspects of modern travel, allowing visitors to stay connected with family and friends, access information, and manage various aspects of their trip. In Fiji, the communication infrastructure has developed significantly, providing travelers with several options to stay connected.

Fiji's telecommunications sector is well-developed, with several service providers offering a range of communication and internet services. The primary telecommunications companies in Fiji are Vodafone Fiji, Digicel Fiji, and Telecom Fiji. These companies provide mobile phone services, internet access, and other communication solutions to both residents and visitors.

Mobile Phone Services

Mobile phone coverage in Fiji is extensive, especially in urban areas and popular tourist destinations. Vodafone Fiji and Digicel Fiji are the two main mobile service providers, offering prepaid and postpaid plans that cater to different needs. Visitors can easily purchase a local SIM card upon arrival in Fiji, either at the airport or from retail outlets and kiosks in towns and cities. To purchase a SIM card, you will need to provide a valid ID, such as a passport.

Prepaid SIM cards are a popular choice for travelers, as they offer flexibility and control over usage. These SIM cards come with a certain amount of credit, which can be used for calls, text messages, and data. You can top up your credit as needed at various locations, including convenience stores, supermarkets, and online. Vodafone Fiji and Digicel Fiji both offer competitive rates and a variety of prepaid plans that include data bundles, making it easy to choose a plan that suits your needs.

Mobile phone reception is generally good in urban areas and tourist hotspots, but coverage may be limited in remote and rural areas. It is advisable to check the coverage maps provided by the service providers to ensure that you will have access to mobile services in the areas you plan to visit.

Internet Access

Internet access in Fiji is widely available, with several options for staying connected. Hotels, resorts, cafes, and restaurants in urban areas and tourist destinations typically offer Wi-Fi access to their guests. However, the quality and speed of Wi-Fi can vary, so it is a good idea to inquire about the internet services when booking your accommodation.

For those who need reliable and high-speed internet access, purchasing a mobile data plan is a practical option. Both Vodafone Fiji and Digicel Fiji offer a range of data plans that can be used with a local SIM card. These data plans provide internet access through the mobile network, allowing you to stay connected wherever there is mobile coverage. The data plans are available in various sizes, from small daily packages to larger monthly bundles, catering to different usage needs.

Another option for internet access is using a portable Wi-Fi device, also known as a pocket Wi-Fi or mobile hotspot. These devices can be rented from telecommunications providers or specialized rental services. A portable Wi-Fi device allows you to connect multiple devices, such as smartphones, tablets, and laptops, to the internet simultaneously. This is particularly useful for families or groups traveling together. The device connects to the mobile network and provides a Wi-Fi signal, ensuring that you have internet access wherever there is mobile coverage.

In addition to mobile data plans and portable Wi-Fi devices, internet cafes are available in urban areas and some tourist destinations. These cafes offer computer terminals with internet access, which can be useful if you need to use a computer for specific tasks. Internet cafes typically charge by the hour or minute, and the rates are usually reasonable.

Telecommunications Providers

Vodafone Fiji is one of the largest telecommunications providers in Fiji, offering a range of mobile, internet, and other communication services. Vodafone Fiji's network covers most of the populated areas in Fiji, providing reliable mobile and internet services to both residents and visitors. The company offers various prepaid and postpaid plans, data bundles, and other services tailored to different needs. Vodafone Fiji also provides roaming services, allowing visitors to use their home country SIM cards while in Fiji, although this can be more expensive than using a local SIM card.

Digicel Fiji is another major telecommunications provider in Fiji, offering similar services to Vodafone Fiji. Digicel Fiji has a wide network coverage and provides competitive rates for mobile and internet services. The company offers a range of prepaid and postpaid plans, data bundles, and other services designed to meet the needs of travelers. Digicel Fiji also provides roaming services for international visitors.

Telecom Fiji is primarily a provider of fixed-line and broadband internet services. While Telecom Fiji's services are more focused on residential and business customers, the company also offers Wi-Fi hotspots in various locations, providing an additional option for internet access.

Practical Tips for Staying Connected

1. Purchase a Local SIM Card: Buying a local SIM card is one of the most cost-effective ways to stay connected in Fiji. Prepaid SIM cards are widely available, and you can choose a plan that suits your needs.

2. Check Coverage: Before purchasing a SIM card or data plan, check the coverage maps provided by the telecommunications companies to ensure that you will have access to services in the areas you plan to visit.

3. Use Wi-Fi When Available: Take advantage of Wi-Fi available at hotels, resorts, cafes, and restaurants to save on mobile data usage. However, be mindful of the security of public Wi-Fi networks and avoid accessing sensitive information.

4. Rent a Portable Wi-Fi Device: If you need reliable internet access for multiple devices, consider renting a portable Wi-Fi device. This can be a convenient and cost-effective option, especially for families or groups.

5. Top Up as Needed: If you are using a prepaid SIM card, keep track of your credit and top up as needed. Topping up is easy and can be done at various locations, including convenience stores, supermarkets, and online.

6. Use Internet Cafes: In urban areas and some tourist destinations, internet cafes provide a useful option if you need to use a computer with internet access. Rates are usually reasonable, and these cafes often offer printing and other services.

7. Stay Informed: Keep informed about any updates or changes to telecommunications services in Fiji by checking the websites of the service providers or asking at local outlets.

With multiple service providers offering a range of mobile and internet services, staying connected in Fiji is relatively easy. Whether you choose to use a local SIM card, a mobile data plan, a portable Wi-Fi device, or the Wi-Fi available at your accommodation, there are plenty of options to ensure that you can manage your communication needs while enjoying your stay in this beautiful island nation. By following practical tips and being aware of the available services, you can enjoy seamless connectivity and make the most of your time in Fiji.

Emergency Contacts and Services

When traveling to any country, it is crucial to have information about emergency contacts and services readily available. In Fiji, knowing who to call and where to go in case of an emergency can make a significant difference in ensuring your safety and well-being. This detailed explanation will cover the emergency contacts and services available in Fiji, including medical assistance, police services, fire services, and other important resources. By understanding these services and having the necessary contact information, you can be better prepared for any unexpected situations during your stay in Fiji.

Fiji's emergency services are well-organized and equipped to handle a variety of situations. The main emergency contact number in Fiji is 911. This number can be dialed from any phone, including mobile phones, and will connect you to the appropriate emergency service, whether it be medical assistance, police, or fire services.

Medical Assistance

Fiji has a network of hospitals, clinics, and medical centers that provide healthcare services to residents and visitors. In case of a medical emergency, you can call 911 to request an ambulance or immediate medical assistance. The following are some of the major hospitals and medical facilities in Fiji:

1. **Colonial War Memorial Hospital (CWMH)**: Located in Suva, the capital city, CWMH is the largest public hospital in Fiji. It provides a wide range of medical services, including emergency care, surgery, and specialized treatments. The hospital is well-equipped and staffed by experienced medical professionals.

2. **Lautoka Hospital:** Situated in the city of Lautoka on the western coast of Viti Levu, Lautoka Hospital is the second-largest public hospital in Fiji. It offers comprehensive medical services, including emergency care, maternity services, and surgical procedures.

3. **Nadi Hospital:** Located in Nadi, a major tourist hub, Nadi Hospital provides essential medical services, including emergency care, outpatient services, and basic surgical procedures. It is a key medical facility for tourists visiting the western part of Viti Levu.

4. **Labasa Hospital:** Serving the northern division of Fiji, Labasa Hospital is located in the town of Labasa on the island of Vanua Levu. It offers a range of medical services, including emergency care, inpatient services, and specialized treatments.

5. **Private Hospitals and Clinics:** In addition to public hospitals, there are several private hospitals and clinics in Fiji that offer high-quality medical care. Some of the notable private healthcare providers include Oceania Hospitals in Suva and the MIOT Pacific Hospitals, also located in Suva.

Police Services

The Fiji Police Force is responsible for maintaining law and order, preventing and investigating crimes, and ensuring public safety. If you need police assistance, you can call 911 or the local police station. The following are the contact details for some of the main police stations in Fiji:

1. **Central Police Station (Suva):** Located in the capital city, the Central Police Station serves the greater Suva area. It is the main point of contact for police services in the capital and its surrounding regions.

2. **Lautoka Police Station:** This station serves the city of Lautoka and the western division of Viti Levu. It is a key contact point for police services in this region.

3. **Nadi Police Station:** Serving the tourist hub of Nadi, this police station is an important point of contact for visitors requiring police assistance.

4. **Labasa Police Station:** Located in the town of Labasa on Vanua Levu, this station serves the northern division of Fiji.

In addition to these main stations, there are numerous smaller police posts and community policing units throughout Fiji. The Fiji Police Force is committed to ensuring the safety and security of both residents and visitors.

Fire Services

The National Fire Authority (NFA) of Fiji is responsible for providing fire and rescue services throughout the country. In case of a fire emergency, you can call 911 to request assistance from the NFA. The NFA operates fire stations in major towns and cities across Fiji, including Suva, Lautoka, Nadi, and Labasa. The authority is equipped to handle various emergencies, including fire incidents, hazardous material incidents, and rescue operations.

Other Important Contacts and Services

1. Embassies and Consulates: If you are a foreign visitor, it is essential to know the contact details of your country's embassy or consulate in Fiji. Embassies and consulates can provide assistance in case of emergencies, such as lost passports, legal issues, or medical emergencies. Some of the major embassies and consulates in Fiji include the Australian High Commission, the New Zealand High Commission, the United States Embassy, and the British High Commission.

2. Tourist Information Centers: Tourist information centers can provide valuable assistance and information to visitors. These centers offer maps, travel advice, and information about local attractions and services. Tourist information centers are typically located in major towns and cities, including Suva, Nadi, and Lautoka.

3. **Pharmacies and Medical Supplies:** In addition to hospitals and clinics, pharmacies are an essential resource for obtaining medical supplies and medications. Pharmacies are widely available in urban areas and tourist destinations, and many are open extended hours to cater to visitors' needs.

4. **Transport and Towing Services:** In case of a vehicle breakdown or accident, transport and towing services are available to provide assistance. It is advisable to have the contact details of a reliable towing service, especially if you plan to travel to remote areas. Some rental car companies also provide emergency roadside assistance as part of their service.

5. **Travel Insurance Providers:** Having travel insurance is highly recommended when visiting Fiji. Travel insurance can provide coverage for medical emergencies, trip cancellations, lost luggage, and other unforeseen events. It is essential to carry the contact details of your travel insurance provider and understand the procedure for making a claim in case of an emergency.

Practical Tips for Emergency Preparedness

1. **Save Important Contacts:** Save the contact numbers for emergency services, your embassy or consulate, and your travel insurance provider on your mobile phone. It is also a good idea to have a written copy of these contacts in case your phone is not accessible.

2. **Know Your Location:** Be aware of your surroundings and know the address of your accommodation. In case of an emergency, providing accurate location information can help responders reach you quickly.

3. **Stay Informed:** Keep informed about local news and weather conditions, especially if you are traveling to remote or rural areas. Being aware of potential risks can help you take appropriate precautions.

4. **Carry Identification:** Always carry a form of identification, such as your passport or a copy of it, and any important medical information, such as allergies or chronic conditions.

5. **Have a Basic First Aid Kit:** Carry a basic first aid kit with essential supplies, such as bandages, antiseptic wipes, pain relievers, and any personal medications you may need.

6. **Stay Calm and Follow Instructions:** In case of an emergency, stay calm and follow the instructions of local authorities and emergency responders. Cooperating with them can help ensure your safety and the safety of others.

Being prepared and informed about emergency contacts and services in Fiji is essential for ensuring your safety and well-being during your visit. By knowing who to call and where to go in case of an emergency, you can handle unexpected situations more effectively. Whether you need medical assistance, police services, or fire services, Fiji's emergency infrastructure is well-equipped to provide the necessary support. Additionally, having the contact details of your embassy or consulate, travel insurance provider, and other essential services can further enhance your preparedness. By following practical tips and staying informed, you can enjoy a safe and memorable experience in the beautiful islands of Fiji.

CHAPTER 14

DAY TRIPS AND EXCURSIONS

Fiji is a paradise of natural beauty and vibrant culture, offering an array of day trips and excursions that provide travelers with unforgettable experiences. Whether you're looking to explore lush rainforests, pristine beaches, traditional villages, or vibrant marine life, Fiji has something for everyone.

One of the most popular day trips in Fiji is visiting the Mamanuca Islands. This group of islands is renowned for its stunning white-sand beaches, crystal-clear waters, and vibrant coral reefs. Day trips to the Mamanucas often include activities such as snorkeling, diving, and swimming, allowing you to experience the incredible underwater world. Many tour operators offer boat trips to the islands, providing transportation, snorkeling gear, and lunch. A visit to the Mamanuca Islands is perfect for those looking to relax on beautiful beaches and explore the vibrant marine life.

For a unique cultural experience, consider a day trip to Navala Village. Located in the highlands of Viti Levu, Navala Village is one of the last remaining traditional Fijian villages with thatched-roof houses. A visit to Navala offers a glimpse into the traditional Fijian way of life, with opportunities to meet the villagers, learn about their customs, and participate in a traditional kava ceremony. The village is surrounded by stunning mountain scenery, making the journey to Navala as memorable as the destination itself.

Another excellent day trip is exploring the Coral Coast, which stretches along the southern coast of Viti Levu. The Coral Coast is known for its beautiful beaches, lush rainforests, and vibrant coral reefs. Popular activities on the Coral Coast include snorkeling, diving, and visiting local attractions such as the Kula Eco Park, where you can see a variety of native Fijian wildlife. The Coral Coast is also home to several traditional villages where you can learn about Fijian culture and history. A day trip to the Coral Coast offers a mix of relaxation and adventure, with plenty of opportunities to explore the natural beauty and cultural heritage of Fiji.

If you're interested in exploring Fiji's natural wonders, consider a day trip to the Sigatoka Sand Dunes National Park. Located near the town of Sigatoka, this national park features impressive sand dunes that rise up to 60 meters high. The park offers several hiking trails that allow you to explore the dunes and enjoy panoramic views of the coastline. The Sigatoka Sand Dunes are also an important archaeological site, with ancient artifacts and pottery fragments found in the area. A visit to the Sigatoka Sand Dunes National Park provides a unique opportunity to explore one of Fiji's most striking natural landscapes.

For those who love adventure, a day trip to the Navua River is a must. The Navua River, located on the island of Viti

Levu, offers exciting opportunities for river rafting and kayaking. The river winds through lush rainforests and deep gorges, providing a thrilling and scenic adventure. Many tour operators offer guided rafting trips that include transportation, equipment, and lunch. The Navua River is also home to several waterfalls, which you can visit as part of your river adventure. A day trip to the Navua River is perfect for adrenaline seekers and nature lovers alike.

Another fantastic day trip destination is the Garden of the Sleeping Giant, located near Nadi. This beautiful garden was founded by the late actor Raymond Burr and is home to a vast collection of orchids and tropical plants. The garden offers walking trails that wind through lush landscapes, providing a peaceful and relaxing experience. A visit to the Garden of the Sleeping Giant is a great way to escape the hustle and bustle of Nadi and enjoy the natural beauty of Fiji.

For a truly unique experience, consider a day trip to Cloud 9, Fiji's floating platform located in the Mamanuca Islands. Cloud 9 offers a one-of-a-kind experience, allowing you to relax on a floating bar and pizzeria surrounded by the turquoise waters of the South Pacific. The platform features sun loungers, day beds, and a wood-fired pizza oven, making it the perfect place to unwind and enjoy the stunning scenery. You can also snorkel and swim in the clear waters around Cloud 9, making it a great destination for both relaxation and adventure.

The island of Taveuni, known as the Garden Island, is another excellent destination for a day trip. Taveuni is famous for its lush rainforests, waterfalls, and diverse wildlife. One of the highlights of Taveuni is the Bouma National Heritage Park, which features several beautiful waterfalls and hiking trails. The Lavena Coastal Walk is a popular trail that takes you through pristine rainforest and along the coastline, ending at a stunning waterfall. Taveuni is also home to the Somosomo Strait, one of the best diving spots in Fiji, where you can explore vibrant coral reefs and encounter a variety of marine life. A day trip to Taveuni offers a perfect blend of adventure and natural beauty.

Another memorable day trip is visiting the Fijian island of Malolo Lailai. This island is part of the Mamanuca group and is known for its beautiful beaches and clear waters. Malolo Lailai offers a range of activities, including snorkeling, diving, and kayaking. You can also relax on the island's pristine beaches and enjoy the stunning views of the surrounding ocean. Several resorts on Malolo Lailai offer day passes, allowing you to enjoy the island's facilities and amenities for a day. A visit to Malolo Lailai provides a perfect escape from the mainland and a chance to experience the idyllic beauty of Fiji's islands.

For those interested in marine life, a day trip to the Yasawa Islands is highly recommended. The Yasawa Islands are known for their stunning coral reefs and abundant marine life, making them a popular destination for snorkeling and diving. One of the highlights of the Yasawas is the Sawa-i-

Lau Caves, a series of limestone caves that you can explore by swimming through underwater tunnels. The Yasawa Islands also offer beautiful beaches, clear waters, and a relaxed atmosphere, making them an ideal destination for a day trip. Several tour operators offer boat trips to the Yasawas, providing transportation, snorkeling gear, and lunch.

Finally, a day trip to the capital city of Suva offers a chance to explore Fiji's vibrant urban culture. Suva is home to a range of attractions, including the Fiji Museum, which showcases the country's rich history and cultural heritage. The city also offers a variety of markets, shops, and restaurants, where you can sample local cuisine and shop for souvenirs. A visit to the Suva Municipal Market is a must, where you can find fresh produce, handmade crafts, and traditional Fijian foods. Suva also offers beautiful parks and gardens, such as the Thurston Gardens, providing a peaceful escape from the bustling city.

In conclusion, Fiji offers a wealth of day trips and excursions that cater to a variety of interests and preferences. From exploring stunning islands and coral reefs to experiencing traditional Fijian culture and enjoying thrilling adventures, there is something for everyone in this beautiful island nation. By planning your day trips and excursions carefully, you can make the most of your time in Fiji and create unforgettable memories. Whether you're looking to relax on pristine beaches, hike through lush rainforests, or dive into the vibrant underwater world, Fiji's diverse landscapes and rich culture provide endless opportunities for exploration and adventure.

CONCLUSION

As you reach the end of this comprehensive guide to exploring Fiji, we hope you feel equipped with the knowledge and inspiration to embark on your own adventure in this stunning island paradise. Fiji is a land of remarkable diversity, offering everything from breathtaking natural landscapes and vibrant coral reefs to rich cultural experiences and warm, welcoming communities.

Throughout this guide, we've dug into the best places to visit, the most exciting activities to partake in, and the essential information needed to make your trip both safe and enjoyable. Whether you're planning to relax on pristine beaches, explore lush rainforests, immerse yourself in local traditions, or indulge in luxury accommodations, Fiji offers a wealth of opportunities to create unforgettable memories.

Fiji's beauty lies not just in its landscapes but also in its people. The Fijian spirit of hospitality, friendliness, and community is something that every traveler will cherish. By visiting local villages, participating in traditional ceremonies, and supporting local artisans, you contribute to preserving and celebrating Fiji's unique culture and heritage.

Remember, preparation is key to a successful trip. From understanding visa requirements and local customs to knowing the best times to visit and the essential items to pack, being well-informed will ensure that your journey is smooth and enjoyable.

We encourage you to embrace every moment of your Fijian adventure. Take the time to connect with nature, engage with the locals, and immerse yourself in the diverse experiences that Fiji has to offer. Each island, each village, and each person you encounter will add a unique flavor to your journey.

As you explore Fiji, keep in mind the importance of sustainable and responsible travel. Respect the natural environment, support local businesses, and be mindful of the cultural practices and traditions of the communities you visit. By doing so, you contribute to the preservation of Fiji's natural and cultural treasures for future generations to enjoy.

Thank you for choosing this guide as your companion in planning your Fijian adventure. We hope it has provided you with valuable insights and practical tips to make your trip truly special. May your journey to Fiji be filled with joy, discovery, and wonderful memories that will last a lifetime.

Vinaka vaka levu (thank you very much) and safe travels!

Printed in Great Britain
by Amazon